The Witch's Athame

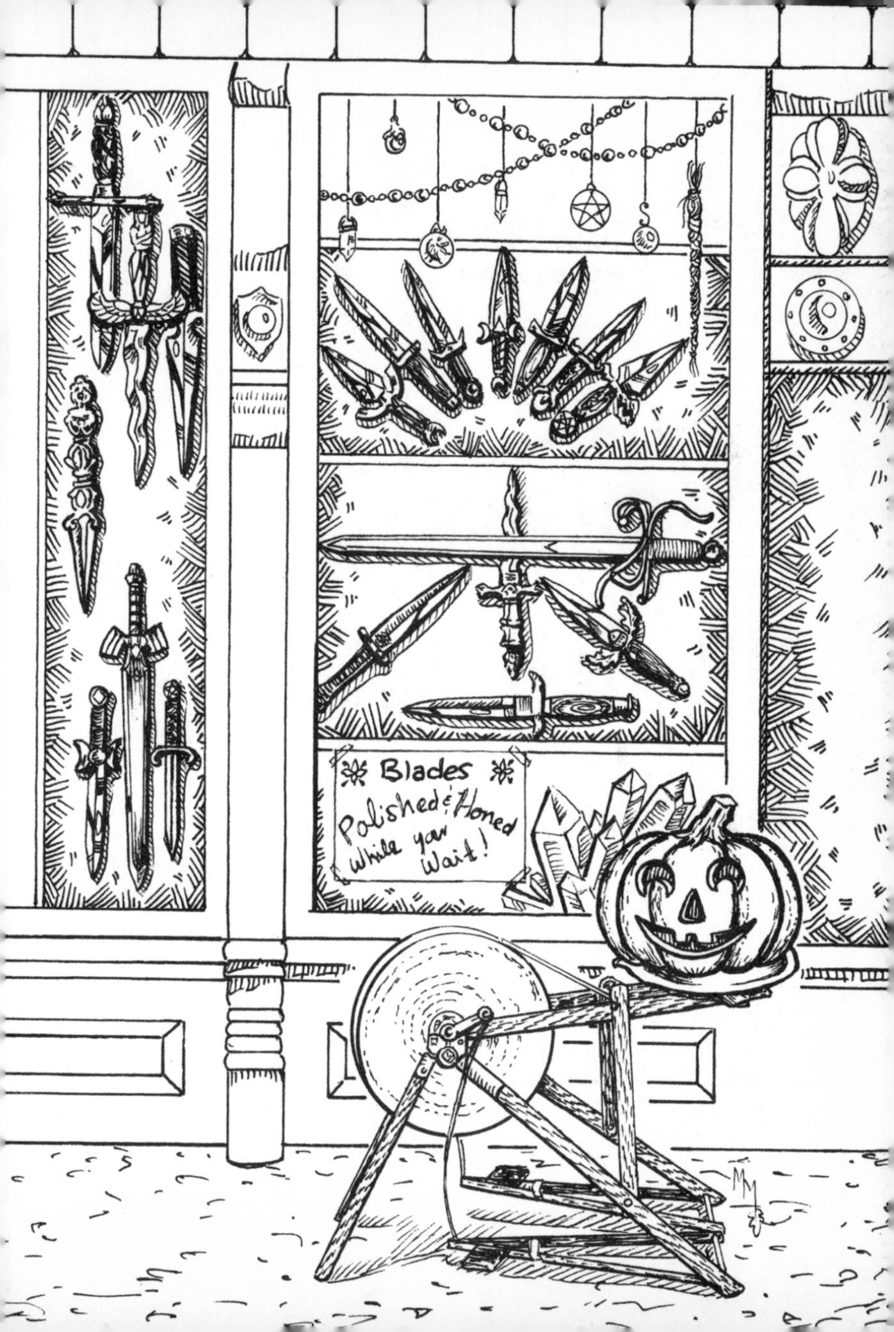
Blades
Polished & Honed
While you Wait!

photo by Tyrnn Urban

Jason Mankey has been a Pagan and a Witch for over twenty years and has spent much of that time writing, talking, and ritualizing across North America. He's a frequent visitor to a plethora of Pagan festivals, where he can often be found talking about Pagan deities, rock and roll, and various aspects of Pagan history. He is currently the editor of the Patheos Pagan channel and can be found online at his blog, *Raise the Horns*.

The Craft, Lore &
Magick of Ritual Blades

The
Witch's
Athame

Jason Mankey

Llewellyn Publications
Woodbury, Minnesota

First Edition
First Printing, 2016

Book series design by Rebecca Zins
Cover design by Lisa Novak
Cover illustration by John Kachik
Interior illustrations by Mickie Mueller

Llewellyn Publishing is a registered trademark of
Llewellyn Worldwide Ltd.

Library of Congress Cataloging-in-Publication Data
Names: Mankey, Jason.
Title: The witch's athame : the craft, lore & magick of ritual blades /
Jason Mankey.
Description: FIRST EDITION. | Woodbury : Llewellyn Worldwide, Ltd,
2016. | Series: The witch's tools series; # 3 | Includes bibliographical
references.
Identifiers: LCCN 2015039070 (print) | LCCN 2015040836 (ebook) |
ISBN 9780738746784 | ISBN 9780738748177
Subjects: LCSH: Witchcraft. | Swords—Folklore. | Knives—Miscellanea.
Classification: LCC BF1566 .M2765 2016 (print) | LCC BF1566 (ebook)
| DDC 133.4/3—dc23
LC record available at http://lccn.loc.gov/2015039070

Llewellyn Publications
A Division of Llewellyn Worldwide Ltd.
2143 Wooddale Drive
Woodbury, MN 55125-2989
www.llewellyn.com
Printed in the United States of America

To my wife, Ari:
you make everything possible.
And to my dad: thanks for always
believing. Love you both!

contents

Contents

introduction

When I began my journey into Witchcraft, I was initially bothered by the athame. Why would a nature religion feature a knife as one of its primary working tools? The symbol of the pentagram, the chalice (or cup), and the broom all made sense to me, but a knife? I associated the knife with negative things; the act of cutting is as destructive as it is useful, after all. As a result of my uncomfortableness with the athame, it was a few years before one found a place on my altar.

When I look back on my initial reluctance to adopt the athame as a working tool, I find myself rather embarrassed. Like the broom and the cup, the knife is a common household instrument. My kitchen has over twenty knives in it, ranging from butter knives to steak knives. While many Witches own elaborate athames, a simple knife is just as effective as a more decorated one. I have one athame that looks as if it belongs in a box with my camping supplies.

In some ways the athame is the modern tool of the Witch. Wands, cauldrons, and brooms have been associated with Witchcraft for thousands of years, but knives not so much. The word *athame* is of relatively recent vintage too, first showing up in print in 1949. While the word athame may not be particularly old, knives have a long history of use in both magick and ritual. After researching that history, I think the odd thing would be *not* having a knife on the Witch's altar.

The athame can often be the source of controversy. There are some who say that it should never be used for physical cutting, and others who treasure it specifically for its practical applications. Like most things tied to Witchcraft, proper use of the athame depends on the practitioner. If it feels right to the Witch "doing the doing," then the athame is being used properly. Besides, there's no rule that says a Witch can own only one athame. I keep one in the kitchen and one on the ritual altar.

Along with my sword, my athames are among my most prized magical possessions. I use the athame during ritual, but also for divination. When I cook or bake my "cakes" for the ceremony of cakes and ale (or wine), I often use my athame as a kitchen utensil. I find that it puts a little extra energy into my goodies. The athame is both a practical tool and a spiritual one; its magick brings me closer to the Lord and the Lady and those who have left this world before me.

For those who are just beginning their journey into Witchcraft, I hope this book answers any questions you might have about the athame. The path of the Witch is one of continual discovery. Here's hoping that my more traveled friends find something new to them in these pages.

Anatomy of an Athame

To put it simply, an athame is a knife dedicated to magical purposes. Certain traditions mandate the size of the blade and a few other factors, but outside of those specific traditions athames are made from all sorts of materials and come in various sizes. Before delving too deeply into the lore of the athame, it might be a good idea to go over the various components that make up the average athame.

Blade: The blade is the knife's cutting surface. The average athame blade is made from steel, but several other materials can be used instead. Some of the more common are crystal, stone, wood, and even bone! If it works for you and has a pointy end, it will make a fine athame.

Hilt: Another name for hilt is handle; this is the part of the athame you pick up and hold in your hand. Many hilts are made of wood, but like the blade, they can be made from nearly any material.

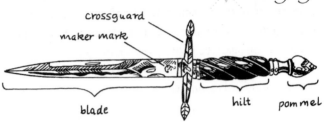

Detail of knife

crossguard

maker mark

blade

hilt

pommel

Crossguard: The crossguard is where the blade and the hilt meet, and is sometimes called a *handguard*. On most athames today, the crossguard is both ornamental and practical. If you aren't paying attention, it keeps your hand from sliding onto the blade. My favorite athame has a crossguard in the shape of two oak leaves.

Pommel: Located at the end of the knife, the pommel is often a raised or rounded end piece. Pommels can be decorative and/or elegantly functional.

Maker Mark: Many blades come with a small symbol already upon them. This is a maker mark, and is generally left by the craftsperson or company that made the knife.

Scabbard: The scabbard isn't a part of the athame, but it's what the athame can be placed in. It's a sheath for the blade. Some athames come with a scabbard, but many do not. Scabbards can be made from just about anything but are usually made from leather, metal, or wood.

Pronouncing the Word Athame

The pronunciation of the word *athame* varies from place to place and country to country. Witchcraft was initially an initiatory tradition, with its rites and rituals passed from teacher to student, but over the last fifty years it has become more of a "book" tradition. Since most early books on modern Witchcraft didn't come with a pronunciation guide, people would run into the word athame while reading and then settle on a personal way of pronouncing it. Eventually some of those various pronunciations became common, and most geographic areas have settled on a particular way of saying the word.

In England the word is pronounced "uh-thah-MEE," and this is probably the original pronunciation of the word. There are various theories on how modern Witchcraft developed, but one thing most people believe is that it began in Great Britain, most specifically England. I once saw a bumper sticker that said "I gave him a whammy with my athame!" which is how I remember the English pronunciation.

I first encountered Witchcraft in the Midwest, where the word is generally pronounced "ATH-uh-may." Before hearing anyone else say the word, this is how my brain interpreted the word and it's still the pronunciation I generally use today. After practicing Witchcraft for many years in the Midwest, my wife and I moved to Northern California, where the word is generally pronounced "ahh-thah-MAY." At this point in my life I generally use the both the Midwestern and West Coast pronunciations interchangeably, though my wife steadfastly sticks to the Midwestern version.

I've also heard athame pronounced as a two-syllable word. When this is done, it generally comes out as "ahh-THAME." The two-syllable pronunciation is the rarest of the various ways athame is pronounced, but it's certainly not wrong. No matter how you pronounce the word, most Witches will know exactly what you are talking about, and I've rarely (if ever) encountered a friendly Witch who corrected someone on their pronunciation of athame.

That being said, I did run into a very unfriendly Witch who liked to "correct" people on how to pronounce the word when they visited her shop. One afternoon while visiting she said to me, "In my very old tradition it's pronounced 'ahh-thah-MAY.'" Without missing a beat, I looked back at her and said, "In my two-thousand-year-old tradition it's pronounced 'ATH-uh-may.'" As far as I know she never corrected anyone ever again, and no, my tradition is not really two thousand years old, but it was fun to say!

Finding an Athame

A friend of mine bought me my first athame. He had seen me admiring it at my local Witch store and surprised me with it a few days later. It wasn't the perfect traditional athame, but it was the perfect athame for me at that particular point in time. Traditionally the athame is a straight, double-sided, five-inch blade with a (black) wooden hilt, but mine was far from that.

Instead of having a straight cutting surface, my athame had a wavy blade, and was about seven inches long. It had a brown wooden handle with a male face on the pommel (the rounded end of the handle) that reminded me of the Greenman. Old Wavy came with an ornate wooden sheath that always provided a rather dramatic sound and look when drawing him out for use in ritual. I've never seen another Witch with an athame like my first one, but I was smitten with him the first time I held him. (I tend to name my athames; I'm not sure if that's normal behavior.)

Most things radiate energy. Often that energy is subtle, but a good Witch nearly always picks up on it. When deciding whether to purchase or use a ritual tool, it's important to "sense" that energy. If you pick up an athame and it doesn't quite feel right in your hands, you shouldn't purchase that athame. The metal, the wood, the conditions it was created in—all of that is going to have an effect on the energy attached to that particular knife. Old Wavy was manufactured in China and was most certainly not created with the express purpose of being an athame, but he felt just right in my hands.

My wife had a similar experience when purchasing her third athame. We were at a local Pagan gathering and she stopped to look at some blades in the vendor room. At the third table we stopped at, she saw a very traditional athame and just had to get a closer look at it. As it was a pretty expensive piece (two hundred dollars—Old Wavy was about forty bucks), the vendor had to pull it out of a locked case before my wife could examine it.

The second she picked up that knife, she said "oh" and her eyes got bigger. It wasn't an exceptionally large athame, but it felt so much heavier than it looked. That blade had a presence and a weight that could only be explained by just how much energy was attached to it. When my wife heard the seller's asking price, she handed the blade back to the vendor, but even though the athame had left her hand, it hadn't left her heart.

She continued to talk about it as we strolled through the vendor room, and she brought it up again later after we returned to our hotel room. Finally I looked at her and told her to just go buy the thing, so we headed back down to merchant's row. As fate would have it, "her" blade was still there waiting for her, like I knew it would be.

When purchasing an athame, it's important to be comfortable with the asking price. It's said to be bad luck to haggle over the price of a magical tool. If it's too expensive for you, no worries; you either weren't meant to have it or weren't meant to have it at that particular time. The perfect tools always come along at the perfect time.

Wavy knife

9

I'd love for my athame story to have ended with me being completely happy with Old Wavy and walking off into the moonlight with him, but that wasn't the case. A wavy blade is considered "wrong" in some Witchcraft traditions, including the one I signed up for. Such things were never said aloud to me, but in my tradition blades are traditionally double-edged, with a black handle. My blade did not have a double edge nor a black handle. In order to meet the requirements of my tradition, I would have had to purchase or make a new blade.

Making a new blade was not possible; there was no way my wife was going to let me play with fire and red-hot pieces of metal. I settled for buying a rather ordinary knife with a two-sided blade off the Internet. As far as athames go, it was (and is) perfectly serviceable, but it didn't really feel like an extension of myself. I even lost it for about ten months, but that loss never really bothered me. It was clear that my "serviceable blade" wasn't going to cut it at as my primary working tool.

Acorn knife

11

Six months before I began writing this book, I found a lovely athame online that looked absolutely perfect for me. It was double-sided and had the required black handle, but that was only the beginning. Its silver blade emerged from an acorn on the crossguard, flanked by two gold oak leaves, with the pommel also in the shape of an acorn. As the name of my coven is the Oak Court, an "acorn knife" felt particularly apt. It was something I had been hoping to receive as a gift at Yuletide, but since it was a custom-made piece, the wait time on my athame was five months. It ended up being a very long five months.

About a month after receiving my acorn athame, my serviceable brown-hilted knife was returned to me. I was actually happy to see it again, and its return coincided nicely with the writing of this book. Nearly all of the "athame experiments" written about in this book were done on my once "orphaned" blade. It will never be my primary athame, but at least I like working with it now.

Why a Knife? The Practicality and the Inconvenience of the Athame

It's easy to find reasons to be uncomfortable with knives. Outside of the dinner table and camping trips, knives are generally seen as weapons, but that's a rather recent development. As we've moved further and further away from our agrarian roots, we've had less need for knives in general, but for most of history knives have been an integral part of day-to-day human existence. People used them for a variety of purposes, and they were an extremely common and handy tool.

As a boy (and a Boy Scout), I owned several knives growing up. My favorite was an old pocketknife that I used for a variety of camping activities. I cut rope with it, whittled sticks with it, and even used it for cutlery when eating dinner. It was a constant companion and something that I thought I literally couldn't live without while in the woods.

For centuries there were many people who really couldn't live without a knife. They used knives to kill and clean game, cut down branches for shelter, and harvest food. Most pioneers didn't own guns, but I'm guessing that the majority of them owned a knife. We live in an era where most of us don't hunt our own food or go out into the wilderness for days and weeks at a time. Seeing someone with anything other than a kitchen knife today is sometimes unsettling, but that's a relatively recent phenomenon.

The tools of a Witch, above all, are practical. Sixty years ago, a random knife on a small table (altar) was unlikely to elicit much comment. Today it's probably a bit more noticeable if your athame is more ornate than a steak knife, but the beginnings of every tool used by the Witch are rooted in practical application. The cup, the broom, even a dish of salt—these are all common items that can be used for a variety of purposes.

Because knives can be used as weapons, various states and countries have laws prohibiting their use in public. If you are a public Witch, be sure to check your state and local laws to see whether it's legal to use a metal blade in a public space (such as a park). Some places even restrict how a knife can be transported in public. If you have to take your athame with you somewhere, it's best to keep it in your car's trunk and wrapped in a small towel or blanket.

Many Pagan festivals and Pagan-friendly places like Renaissance fairs allow steel blades to be worn if they are "peace-bonded." A peace-bonded weapon is one that is tied into its scabbard so that it can't be drawn. In such instances the sword or knife in question is more of a decorative prop than a magical tool. At some of the indoor Pagan festivals I attend, athames are allowed during ritual but not in other public spaces, and they have to be wrapped up when walking them through the hotel or convention center.

We've come a long way since the days when knives were common in public spaces. I don't think the restrictions on blades in public spaces are going to change anytime soon (if ever), but it's always worth remembering that knives were common at one point in our history. Just because they are uncommon in a lot of situations today doesn't mean they were looked at that way one hundred years ago. The knife has a long and mostly noble history, and because of that our athames should sit proudly on our altars and rest mightily in our hands.

GETTING TO THE POINT
Angus McMahan

FROM 1996–1998, I was the manager of the first witchy store in Santa Cruz County, called 13: Real Magick. In sight of the front door (but strategically at the rear of the store) was the athame case. It was only three feet high—just a small glass-fronted hutch—and it only had space for about eight normal-size blades, if you crammed 'em in, Tetris fashion.

But that little display of glittering prizes was magnetic.

A person would enter our store for the first time and give the place a quick overlook, and then their gaze would fall on those two mirrored shelves—that reflected the BLADES. And our guest would get this sleepy, intense, thoughtless, lustful look on their face. They would stagger through the store, heedless of my greeting (as well as the herbs, books, and incense to their port and starboard), intent only on getting closer—immediately—to the KNIVES. Oh ... MY ...

And then, just as quickly, their interest would cease after only a cursory perusal of the athames.

We didn't have their athame. The one for them.

The one.

For no other tool in the basic altar kit is as deeply personal, as receptive, as mutual, as a Witch's athame. (I suppose there is an argument to be made for wands, but this was the '90s, and athames reigned supreme in that pre-Hogwarts era.)

Our customers never lingered at the tiny knife hutch. A quick glance would suffice. Is mine here? No. Okay. Someday... soon, maybe...

But every so often, the blade and its owner would find each other. And then the attraction would be downright primal. My employees and I learned to be quick with the keys when we saw this reaction. And sometimes it was difficult to get the Witch to stand back so we could unlock the little glass doors; we were between them and their blade!

And then, the tenderness... the focus... the weighing and balancing... It was almost too personal to witness, like a teenager's first kiss.

We learned that we could charge almost anything for an athame. Once the knife and its owner had connected, well then, here's-all-my-money, I have to GO. NOW.

The dirty little retail secret was that the athame case was not a big moneymaker, even with some elevated mark-up on our part. Sales were always slow. Dramatic, intimate, but few and far between. And maddeningly, the connections that were made were always beyond any trends or fashion—so buying the athames from our suppliers was fairly arbitrary. You just never knew what blade was going to click with what Witch.

And we acquired only good-quality, black-handled, double-sided blades to begin with, so our wholesale investment was substantial for each knife. Our favorite suppliers were the ones who touted "no minimum order."

Cleaning the athame case was always a bit of a chore. For one thing it was small and low to the ground. To play with the knives you had to kneel before the case, which seemed appropriate. But to dust all that mirror and black-handledness was a delicate (and frequent) affair.

And, retail secret here: We often found that we were removing more than just fingerprints, because sometimes our guests would place psychic "holds" on various blades if they couldn't afford them or were just sloppy with their spellwork. So part of our task list for some days was to wash the athames and freshen their energies.

And don't forget to lock the glass doors when you're done!

Angus McMahan
**All-around word-jockey and
award-winning storyteller •
www.angus-land.com**

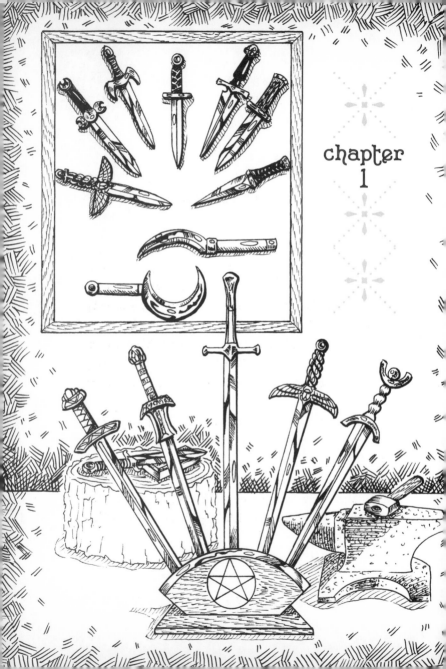

A Short History

The word *athame* is of fairly recent vintage, appearing in print for the first time in 1949. That appearance was not in a how-to or history book, but in a fiction novel, written by Gerald Gardner. *High Magic's Aid* is not a great book, but it's an important one and contains the first somewhat recognizable modern Witch rituals. The athame figures prominently in all of the book's rituals and has been a vital part of modern Witchcraft ever since.

Gardner's inclusion of a ceremonial knife in his text would not have surprised anyone back in 1949; however, his use of the word *athame* most likely would have. Athame as a word didn't exist before Gardner (and/or his initiators), though there are several words that are similar. Most of these "variant spellings" are found in various French translations of the

Key of Solomon. (The *Key of Solomon* is a very influential Italian Renaissance–era grimoire, misattributed to the biblical king Solomon and originally written in Latin.)

The words *artave*, *arthane*, and *arthame* all appear in the many different French translations of the *Key of Solomon*, and they are all probably a garbled mistranslation of the Latin word *artavus*. Artavus doesn't have any deep connection to the realms of magick and Witchcraft, but it does describe a particular type of knife. Artavus was a Medieval Latin word that translates as "penknife" and has been described as a "small knife used for sharpening the pens of scribes."[1]

The 1927 book *The Mysteries and Secrets of Magic* draws heavily from the *Key of Solomon* and includes two words very similar to *athame*. The first appears in an illustration of swords, labeled as an *arthany*. In the same chapter, the author (C. J. S. Thompson) also mentions the *arthana* (knife) as a primary magical tool. Curiously, Thompson's swords are never to be "occupied in any work," while his arthana is used explicitly for the physical act of cutting. He also includes specific instructions for a white-handled knife that most likely influenced the development of the *boline* (see chapter 6).

The word *arthame* shows up in the French book *Witchcraft, Magic, and Alchemy* by Grillot de Givry, which was published

---

1   Sorita d'Este and David Rankine, *Wicca: Magickal Beginnings* (London: Avalonia, 2008), p. 71.

in 1929 (an English translation would show up two years later). De Givry's book most likely had some impact on those interested in the occult because the word *arthame* was subsequently picked up by at least one English writer. In his short story *The Master of the Crabs*, horror writer Clark Ashton Smith uses the word *arthame* to describe a magical knife. Smith's story was released in 1948, just one year before Gardner's *High Magic's Aid*.

There are several other words with spellings close to *athame* that may have influenced Gardner's word choice back in 1949. According to the Oxford English Dictionary, *attame* (or *atame*) is an Old French word that means "to cut or pierce," and might have influenced all the different translation versions of *artavus* that appear in French versions of the *Key of Solomon*.[2] Idries Shah (Arkon Daraul), a contemporary of Gardner and most likely his first biographer, speculated in his book *Secret Societies* (1961) that the word athame might derive from the Arabic term *al-dhamme*, which translates as "blood-letter."[3] Even less likely as a possible origin, but still worth mentioning, is the word *athemay*, which appears in the 1801 work *The Magus*, where the word is used to refer to the sun.

2 James W. Baker, "White Witches: Historic Fact and Romantic Fantasy," in *Magical Religion and Modern Witchcraft*, ed. James R. Lewis (Albany, NY: State University of New York Press, 1996), p. 177.

3 d'Este and Rankine, *Wicca: Magickal Beginnings*, p. 73.

In the end, all or none of these words might have influenced Gardner to choose the word athame for his novel. I'm of the opinion that athame is most likely a misspelling of *arthana,* though there's no way of knowing for sure. It's worth noting that Gardner himself was a fan and collector of knives, even writing a book in 1939 on the Malay *kris* (an Indonesian dagger with a wavy blade). Some of Gardner's critics have used this to suggest that Gardner "made up" the idea of using a magical knife in ritual. On that point they are most definitely wrong.

Knives in Ritual and Religion

Knives have been in existence for millions of years. Before modern humans walked the earth, our genetic ancestors were using knives. No one is quite sure when the first knife was actually used, but estimates range from one million years to perhaps two and a half million years ago. The earliest knives were made of stone and probably used mostly for scraping animal remains.

Modern human beings have been using knives since the beginning of our existence, somewhere between 50,000 and 100,000 years ago. Two bone knives found at the *Grotte de la Vache* ("Cave of the Cow") in Southern France suggest that early humans began using knives for spiritual and religious purposes as early as 12,000 to 15,000 years ago.[4] The two knives found there contain carvings on their blades that seem to reflect spring and autumn. The autumn blade shows a rutting bison, a few seeds, some branches, and a wilting plant. The spring knife contains the figure of a doe and several wavy lines that may imply water.

The bone-knives from Grotte de la Vache are extraordinary for more than the carvings. What makes them really special is that they seem to have never been used for cutting or any other physical purpose. We have no real way of knowing exactly what these knives were used for, but their lack of physical use makes it likely that they were used for some sort of spiritual purpose.

By the year 4500 BCE, knives were being used ceremonially in Pre-dynastic Egypt. Flint knives were used to make sacrifices to the gods and were often elaborately decorated. The Pitt-Rivers knife found in Egypt (named after its owner, English Lieutenant-General Henry Fox Pitt-Rivers), dating from between 3600 to 3350 BCE, was elaborately carved and features over eleven different animals on its blade.[5] Such elaborately carved

---

4   Alexander Marshack, "Exploring the Mind of Ice Age Man," *National Geographic* vol. 147, no. 1 (1975), p. 83.

5   All of the Egyptian material in this chapter comes from a morning spent at the British Museum. Most of the tourists there were taking pictures of the Rosetta Stone, while I spent my time photographing flint knives and placards.

knives were coveted status symbols in ancient Egypt. Knives never used for cutting were often buried with the Egyptian dead.

Bone knife

In Bronze Age Britain (2500 to 800 BCE), daggers were generally buried with the dead. Oddly, the era's other most common tool, the ax, was never buried with the dead. Knives must have had a much higher level of significance. Daggers were also sometimes placed in streams, bogs, and other bodies of water for some sort of undetermined ritual and/or spiritual purpose.

For our purposes, the most significant use of knives in ritual and ceremony comes from the European grimoire tradition. Grimoires (which really just means "magick books") have been around since the ancient Greeks and Egyptians, but really came into their own during the European Renaissance after the advent of the printing press. The most popular and influential grimoire from this period was the *Key of Solomon* (first showing up in Greek in the fifteenth century), and it included a black-handled knife among its working tools.

The *Key of Solomon* wasn't the first book to mention a knife as a working tool. That honor belongs to the *Grimoire of Honorius*, which dates back to the thirteenth century. The rituals contained in texts such as *Honorius* and *Solomon* bear a striking similarity to those of modern Witchcraft. Magick circles are cast and directions are invoked, which means various magicians have been using knives much like we do for at least eight hundred years now, and possibly much longer. Sixteenth- and seventeenth-century Jewish grimoires also reference black-handled knives, and there is some indication that the references date back even further to the eleventh century. Those grimoires did not generally call for the use of a ritual knife, but the sword appears often in the symbolism of the Jewish Kabala.

The black-handled knife appearing in the pages of the *Key of Solomon* meant that its use would merit mention in nearly any treatise on magick and the occult. Books on magick for general audiences have been popular since the invention of the printing press, which means magical knives show up in various odd corners of world history. Joseph Smith, the founder of the Church of Jesus Christ of Latter-Day Saints (the Mormons), used his family's ceremonial dagger to cast magic circles on treasure-hunting expeditions.[6]

Perhaps the most curious reference to the black-handled knife comes from the *Dublin University Magazine* back in 1849, where the following information appears in a footnote:

> A black-handled knife is an indispensable instrument in performing certain rites, and we shall have occasion to describe its virtues by-and-by. It is employed in the ceremonial of Hallow-Eve, and also in the mystic ceremonies performed at the rising of the new moon, as well as in certain diabolic mysteries made use of to include love, etc.[7]

Even if the word athame is of fairly recent vintage, the knife as a magical instrument has a long and distinguished history. Every time we pick up our athames, we are partaking in a religious tradition that stretches back into human pre-history. The knives of our ancestors didn't always look the same as our modern blades, but it's possible that they were being used for similar purposes. It's strange to think about it this way, but the knife might very well be the oldest continually used tool currently on the Witch's altar!

---

6   D. Michael Quinn, *Early Mormonism and the Magical World View* (Salt Lake City, UT: Signature Books, 1998), p. 71.
7   d'Este and Rankine, *Wicca: Magickal Beginnings*, pp. 82–83.

The Black-Handled Knife

Today athame handles come in all sorts of colors and are made from a variety of materials (both natural and synthetic), but traditionally the handle is made of wood and is black. I originally found this to be a strange tradition, but it does have historical precedent and some practical advantages. Much of the black blade's historicity comes from the *Key of Solomon*. Since its original composition, it has remained a staple in the library of most magicians (and even many Witches). Everything in the *Key of Solomon* has been retransmitted numerous times, including references to the black-handled knife.

The use of wood in the hilts of ceremonial daggers was most likely the result of sheer practicality. The majority of daggers made during the Renaissance and Middle Ages had wooden handles. Wood was simply cheaper and more abundant than the alternatives (like metal or ivory). The only odd thing about a "black wooden handle" is that wood generally doesn't come in black. To get a black wooden handle one generally has to paint or stain the blade's hilt.

One of the most intriguing explanations I've read for the black handle is that wooden hilts were generally stained black by the blood of ritual magicians. Apparently many of those magicians were nicking their palms to draw blood for various magical purposes. When that blood was absorbed by the knife's wooden handle, it would turn the hilt black. I've always found that explanation a bit macabre, but it's certainly possible.

The color black has a practical application too: it absorbs energy better than any other color. By using a black-handled knife, the Witch can more easily "set aside" a little energy for later use. The handle isn't going to absorb copious amounts of energy, but sometimes every little bit helps. It's even possible to direct extra energy raised in ritual directly back into the athame. Think of it as a spiritual battery located conveniently in one of your primary working tools!

Why a Doubled-Edged Blade?

I think much of the history of the athame is rather straightforward. As we've seen, knives with black handles have long been a part of the magical tradition. The word athame is a little newer, but there are words quite similar to it dating back centuries. What I've had more trouble with is figuring out exactly why the traditional blade has a double edge.

The grimoire tradition that gave birth to the athame features several different types and styles of knives. Most versions of the *Key of Solomon* feature mainly double-edged blades in their illustrations. When a single-edged blade is shown, it's generally an outlier. The *arthany* pictured in C. J. S. Thompson's more contemporary *The Mysteries and Secrets of Magic* has a curved single-edged blade, and he also includes an equal number of single-edged and double-edged blades.

I think the reason the athame is traditionally double-edged is because the majority of daggers and knives in ritual books were depicted that way. It might also be because a double-edged blade looks more like a mini-sword than a knife with a curved blade. Since the sword and athame are often used interchangeably in ritual, it makes sense for them to be constructed in a similar fashion.

Over the last one hundred years, the definition of *dagger* has come to refer to a double-edged knife with a pointy end. Since ceremonial knives are often called daggers, it makes sense for them to resemble our modern interpretation of the dagger. (There are some traditional daggers with single-edged blades, but those are the exception and are usually found outside of Europe.) Daggers are also often seen as more exciting than the rather utilitarian knife, and what could be more exciting than a ritual blade used for magical work?

There's also a practical reason for the double-edged blade, and it's something I think about every time I consider a curved blade for use as an athame. The athame is designed to project energy. Energy, like most things, takes the path of least resistance. With a double-edged blade, there is no path of least resistance; energy travels equally through every part of the blade. With a single-edged knife, energy is not going to be distributed through the blade equally.

I know many people who use an athame with a single edge and they have no trouble projecting energy and doing good work in circle. However, I think the unequal distribution of energy through the blade would be something I couldn't overcome. It would bug me constantly. If you find a blade you like with a single edge, by all means use it. Just realize that it might give you some trouble when you project energy out of it.

Knife Superstitions

There are a whole host of superstitious beliefs attached to knives, so be careful when giving a knife as a gift or when letting someone else use your athame. Many of the superstitions involving knives are related directly to their use as cutting tools. Receiving the gift of a knife will often result in the severing of a friendship. When a knife is received from a lover, it is a sign that the relationship will soon come to an end.

If someone you love does give you a knife (or a new athame) as a gift, there is a way to reverse the friendship curse. Simply hand the gift-giver a token of appreciation "in payment" for the knife. This is said to restore the bonds that might otherwise have been severed by the knife's blade. It's considered unlucky to close an open pocketknife that has been opened by someone else. Similarly, sheathing a knife you didn't draw is also bad luck.

Knives have also been said to have the ability to affect the weather. As early as 1727, written reports detail how Mediterranean sailors used daggers to break up heavy winds and even ward off tornadoes.[8] I know a few Witches who use their blades while practicing weather magick, and this feels similar.

There's a long tradition of metal objects serving as deterrents against malevolent forces. The best-known object in this category is the "lucky" horseshoe, but knives play into this belief as well. The demons of northern India are apparently so stupid that they will simply run into a naked blade and cut themselves. Knives have also been used throughout Europe to ward off evil spirits. Placing a knife in the bottom of a boat will keep evil spirits away and ensure smooth sailing (or rowing). Filling a large jar with water and placing a knife inside of it is said to repel the Devil. Allegedly, Satan gets so focused on looking at his reflection that he forgets to bother people. Black-handled knives were also used to keep evil Irish fairies at bay as recently as the nineteenth century.

---

8   d'Este and Rankine, *Wicca: Magickal Beginnings*, p. 84.

A Jewish superstition calls for the separation of religious books and iron implements such as knives. Books are thought to preserve lives, while iron ends them. Additionally, knives should never be used to help read a religious text. My athame is often near my Book of Shadows, and they have probably rubbed against each other at least once or twice.

There are several superstitions related to dropping a knife, many of them contradictory. A knife sticking into the ground point first and hilt up can mean good luck or that you will soon be dead. Another legend says that a dropped knife means unexpected company will soon be arriving. The direction in which the dropped knife points will be the direction from which they come. In Finland, there are several "dropped knife" superstitions related to fish. If a knife is dropped while cleaning fish and it points toward the sea, good fishing is assured on the fisherman's next trip. If it points toward land, the next expedition will end in failure.

Not all the superstitions surrounding knives are bad. Placing a knife under the bed of a woman giving birth is said to help with pain, the idea here probably being that the knife will absorb the pain so it no longer troubles the mother-to-be. An athame in tune with a Witch giving birth will probably be even more effective at channeling away some of that pain. In some parts of Europe, knives were placed directly in a baby's crib to ward off evil spirits. (That's one I don't want to try at home.)

In Greece, knives are often placed under pillows to ward off bad dreams. It doesn't sound like the safest practice to me, but if I was being plagued by nightmares, there's nothing I would want more in dreamscape than my athame. In addition to warding off bad dreams, knives in Greece were sometimes used to rid homes of insects. I don't understand the reasoning behind this, unless of course they rid the house of insects by stabbing each one individually.

Because metal was so precious and magical in the ancient world, oaths were often taken upon knives. The next time you or a friend has to "swear to" do something, do it while holding an athame. That will hold both of you to your promise.

Native American Knife Lore

Pagan and magical histories often exclude Native American legends and traditions. It's a serious oversight because modern Witchcraft has been tremendously influenced by Native American spiritualities. All of the Witches out there who use smudge sticks owe their Native American friends a hearty thank-you. In addition, nearly all the information we have about plants and stones native to the Americas initially came from Native Americans.

While I don't know of any traditions involving the athame that came directly from America's first inhabitants, Native Americans do have several interesting legends and customs involving the knife. They've also been using knives nearly as long as Europeans, and have used a wide variety of knife types over the last twelve thousand years, too. Native American knife blades have been made of wood, shell, horn, bone, teeth, copper, and even meteoric iron!

Contrary to popular belief, metallurgy existed in the Americas before the arrival of Europeans. Native metallurgists possessed exceptional skill and were as advanced as their European counterparts; however, most Native American societies used their knowledge to achieve different ends. Empires like that of the South American Inca preferred to craft ornamental items instead of weapons.[9]

One of the reasons we seldom associate America's original inhabitants with metallurgy is that they most often worked with copper. Copper is a beautiful decorative metal and can be quite useful; however, it's a very soft metal. Metal knives became more common in North America once Native Amer-

---

9 Charles C. Mann, *1491: New Revelations of the Americas Before Columbus* (New York: Knopf, 2005), pp. 82–83. Mann's book is endlessly fascinating and one of the most reread books in my house. This is a must-read.

icans had access to iron. Eventually they became quite adept at making knives from bayonet blades, iron files, and other metal scraps.

For Northern California's Hupa tribe (also sometimes spelled Hoopa), knives were a symbol of wealth and social status. Ornate obsidian knives used only in ritual were sometimes up to twenty inches long and two and a half inches wide. If I saw a knife like that in circle, I wouldn't automatically start thinking of social status, but I would be suitably impressed.

Other tribes used knives to indicate social standing too, but the Ojibwe (known by many as the Chippewa) and Sioux of the American West and Midwest wore theirs. Many in these two tribes placed sheathed knives around their necks to indicate wealth. Larger knives indicated greater amounts of wealth. Triangular knives were later worn around the necks of Sioux leaders to indicate rank.[10]

Plains tribes in what is now Missouri used to swear on their knives in a threefold ritual. They'd begin by holding a knife in their right hand raised up toward the sun while reciting an oath. They would then lower the knife and place it between their lips and finally on their tongue.[11]

10 Colin F. Taylor, *Native American Weapons* (Norman, OK: University of Oklahoma Press, 2001), p. 37.
11 Ibid., p. 40.

Perhaps the most fearsome knife (and ceremony) among the natives of North America was known as the Blackfoot Bear Knife Bundle. Common among the Blackfoot (Niitsitapi) tribes, the Bear Knife Bundle featured a large knife with a bear skull attached to the handle. The knives themselves inspired a great deal of fear, and as a result, their owners were largely left alone. Part of that might also be because the initiation ceremony for the Bear Knife Bundle is rather extreme.

To receive a Bear Knife Bundle, the initiate is required to catch the knife when it's thrown at him. After catching the knife, the initiate is then "cast naked upon thorns and held there while painted and beaten thoroughly with the flat of the knife." [12] It's no wonder that individuals who survived the ordeal were given a wide berth in their communities. I'm glad that I avoided such obstacles when I obtained my athame.

Athame Correspondences

Most Witches honor the elements of earth, air, fire, and water and associate many of their magical tools with one of those elements. Often the association between element and tool is obvious. The cup or chalice is designed to hold water, so the

---

12 Clark Wissler, "Ceremonial Bundles of the Blackfoot Indians," *Anthropological Papers* vol. 7, part 2 (New York: American Museum of Natural History, 1912), p. 132.

cup is naturally an expression of water. Incense smoke wafts through the air and thus is associated with the element of air. Salt is used by many Witches for cleansing and is most always linked to the element of earth. Since salt is often mined from the earth, this association makes sense to most of us.

I have always associated the athame (and, by extension, the sword) with the element of fire, but there is some disagreement about this among Witches and other magical practitioners. Depending on the tradition and the individual Witch, the athame is sometimes linked to the element of air. This association comes from the nineteenth-century magical order the Golden Dawn, one of the most important occult orders in history. In the symbology of the Golden Dawn, the wand is considered a tool of fire and the knife of air. Many famous Witches have maintained this association, most notably Doreen Valiente, considered by many to be the "mother of modern Witchcraft."[13]

On some levels, the association with air makes a great deal of sense. Since the athame is rarely if ever used for physical cutting, it must only be cutting through the air. We certainly aren't using our blades to cut through gods or spirits. The element of air is often associated with creativity and communication,

13 Janet and Stewart Farrar, *A Witches' Bible: The Complete Witches' Handbook* (Custer, WA: Phoenix Publishing, 1996), p. 253. Originally published as *The Witches' Way*.

two things that are important during Wiccan ritual. Without a degree of creativity and imagination, we'd be unable to see the magick circle that surrounds so many of us in our rites. Communication is also a vital skill in Witchcraft. If we are unable to articulate our desires, they will never manifest. It's also important that we communicate properly to the entities we want to have join us in circle. If holding an athame makes someone a better communicator, maybe its energies are aligned with air after all.

What element a ritual tool is associated with may not seem all that important in the long run, but how we perceive a tool controls a lot of how we interact with it. I associate my athame with the element of fire because the things I do with it during ritual are linked to modern Witchcraft's perception of that element. When I cast a ritual circle, I'm not just moving around energy; I'm creating a new space between the worlds. There's a line spoken in some circle castings that states: "We are in a time that is not a time and a place that is not a place." When I use my athame to create a circle, I am transforming the space I stand in into something else entirely.

Fire consumes and changes all that it touches. Once something has been touched by flame and heat, it will never be as it once was. When I purify and bless items with my athame, I'm fundamentally changing them. A bowl of salt used in ritual is often purified with the athame; that purification drives all "uncleanliness" from the salt, changing it. I do the same with water, and when I make the consumption of bread and wine truly sacred, I do so by touching them with my athame. For me, the athame is *the* tool of transformation during ritual. Almost everything that changes during my rites as a Witch has been touched by a blade.

Many Witches also view the athame as a tool for channeling one's *magical will*. Magical will is the sum total of our interactions with those around us, the gods, and the earth. When we do positive things, we add to our will. Just like a fire grows when you add more wood to it, the will grows when we engage in positive experiences. We can also add to our magical will by believing in ourselves. A good Witch is determined and steadfast—more qualities that add to one's collective will.

Our actions add to our will, but they are not what allow us to use this personal reserve of energy. To tap into our magical will, we have to believe that magick is a real and powerful force. To utilize will, the Witch has to believe that they are capable of creating change and that they can control that change. Witchcraft is not a science experiment; it's practiced to create specific results. To create "a time that is not a time and a place that is not a place," we have to know that we are capable of such an action. If our will is full of positive energy and we are convinced of our own power, the world opens up and we can manifest change within it.

Because our magical will allows us to create change, it's most often associated with the element of fire, another strong reason to associate the athame with that element. The athame serves as a way to release our true will out into the universe and manifest our desire to walk between the worlds. We use the knife to direct our will because the pointy tip is sharp and precise, just like our will should be in order to practice effective magick.

In addition to linking their tools to the four elements, many Witches also link them to the Goddess and the God and female/male energies. This symbolism is most manifest in the ritual of the *symbolic Great Rite*. The Great Rite is the celebration of two polarities coming together. In many Traditional Witchcraft traditions, this idea is often expressed in the idea of sexual union between a woman and a man. Since sexual coupling is generally not a part of group ritual, the Great Rite is most often celebrated symbolically, with the athame representing the phallus and the cup representing the womb.

In my own personal practice, I don't tend to think of my athame as "masculine"; I think of it as one half of a whole. The creation of new things and energies generally requires at least two forces to unite. To celebrate the mystery of life requires two active principles. In Witchcraft, these principles are often represented by the chalice and the athame. Thinking of an athame as "masculine" doesn't suddenly turn it into a penis; it's still just a tool. But looking at it in such a way helps some to see and experience the truths and mysteries of the natural world. (The Great Rite is explored in more detail in chapter 6.)

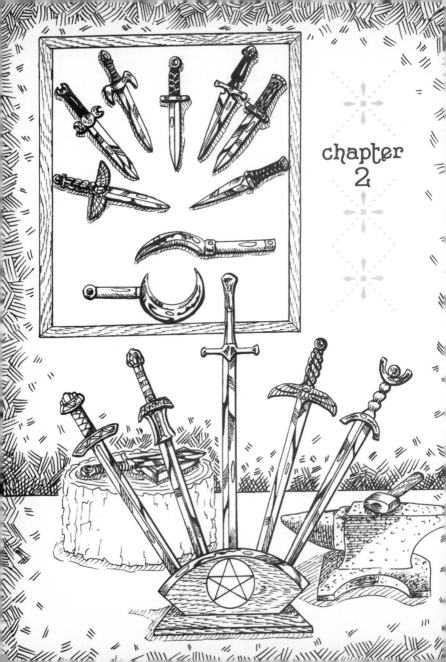

The Other Athames

While most athame blades are made of stainless steel or some other type of metal, an athame can be made of most any material that can be sharpened to a point. The most popular materials outside of metal are generally stone, wood, and bone. I've seen a few athames with plastic blades as well, but unless it's a blade for a young Witchling, it's not something I (and most other Witches) recommend.

As long as you aren't part of a Witch tradition that mandates a certain type of blade during ritual, the materials that can be used to make your athame are nearly limitless. What's most important is that the athame works for (and with) you. If you feel a connection to stone instead of steel, by all means go in that direction. Other than the rule of "an it harm none, do what you will," Witchcraft isn't about do's and don'ts; it's about what works for the individual Witch!

Stone Athames

Human beings have used stone knives for tens of thousands of years. Because of their great antiquity, it's not surprising that many Witches employ an athame made of rock. When I use an athame made of stone, I often feel a deep connection to truly ancient pagan practices. Before all of the great civilizations in history, there were ingenious people using stone knives and tools. When I use an athame made of that material, it's a way of honoring those ancestors.

Stone knives are made through a process known as "knapping," which mostly involves hitting a soft piece of stone with a heavier one. If it sounds labor-intensive, that's because it is! However, it also doesn't require a whole lot of tools or materials. Knapping was one of the first technologies used by human beings and is still being used in many places today.

I've encountered many naturally occurring rocks over the years that are nearly knife-shaped. Such natural athames make for great impromptu tools when doing rituals in the great outdoors. Stone athames (along with wooden ones) also make great alternatives to the traditional steel athame when doing ritual in a public place. If you are doing ritual in a public park, metal knives might not be allowed, but a dull stone knife is usually fine.

An athame of stone has different characteristics than one made of steel. I generally associate stone athames with the element of earth (since that's where they come from), but that can vary depending on the stone being used for the athame. A material such as obsidian, for example, which comes directly from active volcanoes, still has a lot of fire associations.

The more masculine energy generally characteristic of the athame remains in place with most stone blades, but that energy is often tempered with an extra layer of protection. Many of the stones commonly used for athames have a very protective energy, and this is often felt in the energy of a circle cast with a stone blade. For a coven or individual interested in a less masculine athame, a stone such as jade might be a good choice.

Flint knife

Any type of stone can be used to make an athame, but some are more popular than others. Nearly all the stones listed here are commonly used in athames and can be purchased online and at many New Age/metaphysical shops.

Obsidian: Obsidian is a natural form of black glass and is a popular choice for those who prefer an athame made of stone.

The Other Athames

Traditionally, obsidian has been associated with protection, but it also makes a great tool for scrying. Most people scry into mirrors, but if you have an obsidian athame, there's no reason you can't use your blade for the practice. Obsidian knives have been popular for centuries and can still be purchased easily today.

Hematite: Few stones contain more power and energy then hematite, and it's become a popular choice for athames over the last decade. It's a great stone for healing, and an athame made of it can help draw sickness from the body. A hematite athame can be used to help stabilize and balance the energies of a circle. Due to its high iron content, hematite also has strong protective properties.

Quartz Crystal: Quartz is one of the most popular gemstones in modern magick and is increasingly being used for athame blades. Quartz is well known for its ability to amplify magical energy, and its use as a blade naturally complements the athame's primary purpose. Many Witches take advantage of crystal's natural abilities by adding it to the hilts of their athames. I've even heard of a few Witches attaching a piece of crystal to the blade of their knives while casting a circle for a little extra added oomph. Quartz crystal has been used in religious ceremonies all around the world. It's one of humanity's original mystical and magical stones.

Flint: Flint is a great choice for a stone athame in North America because of its extensive use by Native Americans.

Flint was used by Native American shamans for ceremonial purposes and by hunters who used it in spear and arrow points. In both Europe and the Americas, flint was also used to make knives. Flint has long been associated with protection, and when used in an athame, that energy will show up in your circle casting. Flint also has a long history as an aid to starting fires, further connecting the athame to the element of fire.

Chert: Chert (often called *common chert*) is nearly the same chemically as flint but is thought by many to be less "pretty." Like its more popular cousin, chert was one of the first stones used to make knives and is also easy to work with. Many forms of chert contain fossils within them, adding a little extra energy to any athame made of this stone.

Marble: Marble is probably best known as the primary building material of the Romans and the Greeks, but it's been used throughout the world for centuries. Marble is a popular building material because it's easily worked with and durable, two useful qualities for those interested in constructing their own stone athame. Because of its associations with the Greeks, marble is a good choice for the Witch who has an interest in (or relationship with) Hellenic deities.

Petrified Wood: Petrified wood isn't a stone, but it's not quite wood anymore either, so this seemed like the place to include it. What's fascinating about petrified wood is that it's a substance that lives in two worlds. It feels like a stone and yet has the story and energy of something that was once alive. Because of its connection to a living past, an athame made of petrified wood can be used to explore past lives and is a good energy to utilize in rituals (like Samhain) that deal with the dead.

Athames of Wood

Wood is most commonly used in the construction of wands, but it's also a material that makes a great athame. One of my oldest friends in the Craft has exclusively used a wooden athame for over twenty years very effectively. Unlike athames of stone and steel, every bit of a wooden athame has been "alive" at some point in the recent past. That gives wooden athames a very unique energy signature.

What element a wooden athame is representative of really depends on the individual Witch. It's easy to associate a wooden blade with earth; the roots of a tree do grow deeply into the womb of the Great Mother. The traditional association with fire also works as well, but I usually associate wooden athames with the element of air. Most wooden blades are made from branches and not tree trunks. Those branches often "reach up" into the sky and are generally shaken and stirred by a strong breeze.

There are a couple of practical reasons for working with a wooden athame in certain situations. Air is generally a very welcoming element, and casting a circle with a force associated with that element creates a less protective and more inviting circle. (I like to think of it as the "screen door" of ritual circles.) Many Witches work with the *fey* (sometimes called *fairies* and generally a reference to many different supernatural beings that many consider mythological), a people who traditionally don't like iron and steel. Using a steel athame when calling to the fey might result in them ignoring your invitation.

If you choose to work with a wooden athame, it's best to use a knife created from a fallen tree branch. If that's not possible, be sure to "ask" the tree before removing a branch from it. Trees don't usually "speak," but they will often send a pretty clear signal via energy. If the tree you are pinching from gives you the go-ahead to cut down a branch, be sure to thank it when you are done. It's traditional to leave coins, but

I think it makes more sense to leave the tree in question a big drink of water for its roots. It's not just good karma; it makes for good magick.

Wood also provides a powerful way to connect with the local environment. It's much easier to know the "point of origin" with wood than it is with steel or even stone. If your practice is rooted in a deep sense of place, athames made of wood are a good choice.

Because trees have very specific energies and associations, an athame made from one will contain a few "extra properties." If you are looking to undertake a very specific working, a circle cast with a wooden athame might be helpful. Listed here are a few magical woods (which may or may not be common, depending on where you live) that might come in handy during ritual.

Apple: An athame of apple wood adds a little extra magick when performing a love spell. Apples have long been associated with the immortality of the soul and are effective for when an athame is being used to create a portal into the Summerlands.

Ash: In some Nordic traditions, Yggdrasil (the World Tree) was as an ash tree, a perfect association for a wood that many see as a useful tool for traveling between the worlds. Due to this property, ash is an exceptional wood for an athame.

Boxthorn: The "thorn" in the poem "Oak and Ash and Thorn," boxthorn has long been prized for its properties of healing and virility.

Elder: An athame made of elder provides a bit of extra energy when warding off a magical attack or dealing with negative spirits. Ghost hunters would be wise to carry an extra athame made of elder just in case.

Hazel: Hazel has long been used for dowsing rods and is a good choice if you plan to use your athame for divination. It's also traditionally associated with fertility and can give added meaning to the symbolic Great Rite.

Oak: Since this tree is sacred to Druids and long associated with health and protection, an athame made from oak is especially useful for those who work with Celtic deities.

Redwood: Redwood is very soft, which makes it easy to carve an athame out of, but hard to carve symbols into. Redwood is extremely resistant to fire and insects and provides a useful energy when trying to overcome long-term problems. Redwoods are some of the oldest trees in the world and a powerful way to tap into the wild powers of nature.

Walnut: The walnut is a symbol of male virility, and its wood has similar energies. Walnut also increases mental focus and powers, and in recent times has come to be associated with things like telepathy. This is a good wood to use when trying to open up lines of communication.

Yew: Yew trees are poisonous, and because of this, some Witches are wary of them. I believe that the yew's proximity to death makes it an effective wood for Samhain rites and rituals of transition.

Making a Wooden Athame

The number of tools required to make a wooden athame is minimal, and the process from start to finish requires only a few hours. If you choose to make a wooden athame, you'll want to start by rounding up a suitable piece of wood. I suggest using a fallen tree branch instead of a store-bought piece of wood. Whatever you use should feel comfortable in your hand and shouldn't be any thicker than your wrist. You can make your wooden athame as long or as short as you wish, but most wooden athames I've seen over the years have a pretty short blade.

After you find a suitable branch, the most important tool you'll need is a pocket or bowie knife. A bowie knife is sharper and will speed up the process, but pocket knives are far more common and often easier to acquire. You may also want some sandpaper, some tape or ribbon for the hilt, and some wood sealer, but those last items aren't completely necessary.

Start by discarding any parts of the stick you don't need. If your branch is twelve inches long, you'll probably want to get rid of about half the length. Next you'll want to trim off all the bark and any imperfections in the wood, especially any knots that stick out. Your goal here is simply to create a smooth and even piece of wood. When you're done, be sure to mark off an area for your athame's handle. You can make a notch with the knife you are using or make a small mark with a pencil.

Making an athame out of wood requires a lot of whittling, and it sometimes takes a few hours. It's a pretty simple stroke with the pocketknife, similar to peeling a potato. The only difference is that the pressure of each knife stroke should increase with each "whittle" down the stick. When you've got the basic shape down, keep whittling until the blade looks like you want it to. I'm not all that crafty; when making a wooden athame, I'm just hoping for a blade-like shape with a point at the end! Anytime one cuts with a knife, the blade should be moving away from the body. This isn't only for safety; it's the easiest way to use a knife.

When your athame is suitably knife-shaped, you may want to smooth it down a bit with some sandpaper. Sandpaper is especially useful if you want the blade to be completely uniform. Though it's not necessary, I also suggest adding a wood finish to your blade. This will keep it safe from outside elements and give it a shiny look. Alternatively, you can also polish the blade with beeswax for a similar effect.

The Other Athames

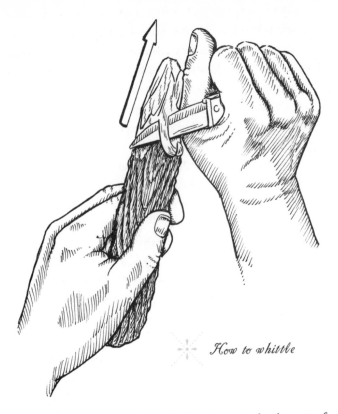

How to whittle

The easiest way to make a hilt is simply to take the part of the branch you marked earlier as the handle and cover it with soft cloth ribbon or tape. Coating the hilt with wood glue and then wrapping cloth ribbon around it is the easiest way to create a working handle. If you've done a good job sanding the handle area (no one wants a splinter during ritual!), painting or staining a hilt onto the blade is also acceptable. Electrical and duct tape are easy ways out here too, but I'm generally wary of industrial-grade plastics.

Once you've got a wrap on the handle, you'll be all done and will have crafted your very own athame. It may not look all that fancy, but it will work in ritual and in whatever magical workings you undertake. As long as you are happy with it, the gods will be happy with it too!

Blades of Bone and Antler

Bone is more likely to be used for the hilt of an athame, but athame blades made from bone aren't unheard of and may be gaining in popularity. Bone knives are ancient, and there is some evidence to suggest that they were used in religious ceremonies 15,000 years ago. Ice Age cave dwellers in what is now modern-day France made bone knives decorated with seasonal motifs and never used those knives for hunting.[14] Could they be the world's oldest athames? Probably not, but it seems likely that they were used for some sort of spiritual purpose.

---

14 Alexander Marshack, "Exploring the Mind of Ice Age Man," *National Geographic* vol. 147, no. 1 (1975), p. 83

I've always found the idea of a bone knife a bit uncomfortable, but I think that's more a reflection of my own personal prejudices. Bone knives offer yet another way to connect with our ancient ancestors and with any spirit animals we might feel close to. If someone has a spiritual bond with a particular animal, wouldn't it make sense for them to use a tool made from that animal? I don't own a bone athame, but I do own a set of deer antlers I wear on occasion, and I find them to be a great way to honor deer and the natural world. Why would a bone blade be any different?

I do think it's wise to be cautious when first using an athame made of bone. Since that bone (or perhaps antler) came from a once-living creature, that animal's spirit may still be hovering nearby. I think it's important to always treat an athame with respect, but perhaps even more so when a piece of that athame came directly from a living creature. I wouldn't want anyone disrespecting the bones of my deceased relatives; the bones of our brothers and sisters in the animal kingdom shouldn't be any different.

Most Witches I know who use bone in their athames either find it in the woods or get their materials from hunters they know to be in touch with the natural world. Most bone blades are not mass-produced but come from artisans who try to honor the spirit of the deceased animal whose parts they are working with. Since bone generally comes to us after an animal dies, the energy in a bone blade is going to be different from that of most other athames. That doesn't make it bad, but only different. If you do end up using a bone athame, proceed with caution until you are used to the energies it emits.

The Secret Athames

In chapter 13 of his 1954 book *Witchcraft Today*, Gerald Gardner wrote:

> It is very amusing to see how clever some witches are in disguising their tools so that they look like something else; indeed, they often are something else, until they are put together in the proper way to be used.

Even today, there are many Witches who must hide and disguise their magical tools for a variety of reasons. Luckily for us, most Witch-tools are easily disguised, and if you find yourself in a situation where using a traditional athame is not possible, you've got lots of options.

My wife became a Witch when she was sixteen years old, and it was something she had to keep secret. She attended a Catholic high school and her mother was (and remains) a very conservative Catholic. When my wife began collecting her magical tools, she decided that the traditional double-sided knife was out of the question, so she sought an alternative.

She eventually settled on a letter opener. Like a more traditional athame, it had a double-sided blade and a wooden handle. Even the letter opener's hilt was black! The only real difference between her letter-opener athame and a more conventional one was the thinness of the blade itself. Her letter-opener athame was so inconspicuous that she could even leave it on the desk in her room without any worry.

When my wife entered college, she ended up living in the dormitory of her university. Weapons were not allowed in her dorm room, so her letter-opener athame came in handy yet again. She used it all throughout college and even beyond because she felt so comfortable with it. Even now, her first athame holds a place of honor on one of our many household altars.

There are other secret athames too. People have been using Swiss Army knives as athames for decades now (it's even mentioned in 1979's *The Spiral Dance* by Starhawk). Most people don't feel threatened by a "knife" that also contains a corkscrew and a bottle opener. For Witches living in the broom closet, a Swiss Army knife athame is a completely inconspicuous choice for use outdoors. I wish I had thought of it back when I was a Boy Scout!

Kitchen knives also work well if you are in a situation where your interest in Witchcraft has to be kept hidden. A steak knife or even a butter knife smuggled out of the kitchen and kept on a nightstand probably won't attract much attention. You can also just put it back in the kitchen when you are done. The downside to using a kitchen knife is that your athame will probably end up getting handled by a lot of different people. If that's acceptable to you, then raid those cupboards!

Toy plastic knives and swords are easy to come by (especially swords), and I've known a few people who have used them as athames over the years. I'm not a big fan of mass-produced, industrialized, polluting plastic as a material for athames, but we do what we have to do sometimes. In dim light, a plastic sword sometimes looks as impressive as the real thing. A Witch must always be practical, and if a plastic knife is the best option available, then go with it.

GETTING TO THE POINT
Lupa

I DIDN'T MAKE my own athame. Because I create art for a living, I'm too close to my work; the energy's too familiar. Don't get me wrong: I love what I do and what I create, and

I've had many people remark on the power in the athames I craft from bone and horn, leather and fur, beads and charms. But when I'm creating a formal ritual, I need to be able to step outside of myself, so I recruit the art of others in my efforts.

The flow of creation is second nature to me at this point, after almost twenty years of making sacred items. I breathe it; I could craft in my sleep. In fact, I've dreamed some of my best ideas, or had them come to me in that liminal state between wakefulness and slumber. And the athames are among some of my most elaborate works, physically and energetically. They pull me in more deeply, challenging me as an artist and a spiritual creator, absorbing more of me than most of the pieces that leave my studio for the wider world.

The blade is almost always bone or horn, usually water buffalo. The handles are more varied: wolf bone, elk antler, coyote femur, stag tine. The hilt and handle are wrapped, sometimes in leather and sometimes in fur and sometimes in bright swaths of braided secondhand yarn. The pommel offers even more opportunities for customization, where beads and feathers and other shiny objects can dangle and gleam.

And what is the blade without its sheath? Deerskin is my usual go-to; it can handle the gentler attentions of dull bone and horn where metal might otherwise slash and tear. Here the theme is continued from the knife itself—maybe silver on black, or red and gold, and often the deep earth tones of the forest, with an antler button to finish it all.

The spirits, too, have their say. I work with hides and bones and the animal spirits within them, listening to their requests and demands, and trying my best to give form to these forces I hold in my mortal hands. I never incorporate a bit of fur or antler until it's ready; every piece of art I make includes the conversation I had with these deceased beings about the care of their remains. I feel the voices thrum in my bones; I hear them in my heart. Every bit of it goes into the knife and sheath, giving them a life not found in mass-produced plastic and steel.

I never know until the end how each athame will look, but I never fail to fall in love. I do know I can't keep them all. So I send them off to other homes, with a prayer to the spirits who once wore these sacred remains, and a wish for a good new afterlife in a sacred place.

Lupa
Author and Artist •
www.thegreenwolf.com

The Other Athames

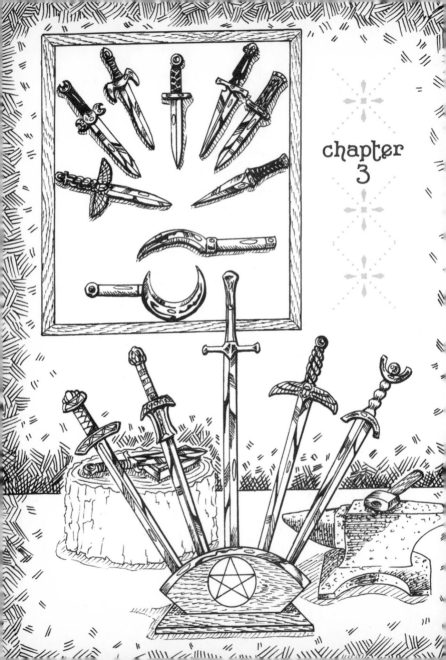

Making an Athame Yours

When I began practicing Witchcraft, I did so as a solitary practitioner. I had no teachers or even friends who were also practicing the Craft. Most everything I did in my early years came directly from books. One of the most influential books in my development as a Witch was *Buckland's Complete Book of Witchcraft* by Raymond Buckland. While I enjoyed *Buckland's Big Blue Book* (a nickname given to the book by many Witches because the book is big and blue!), his bit on the athame always struck me as impractical.

Buckland introduces the athame by saying: "It will not do, then, to simply go to a store and buy a ready-made knife... The best thing, by far, is to make your own from scratch." He then goes on to give instructions for constructing one's own athame, calling for tools like a grinding wheel and a bandsaw. For a twenty-one-year-old kid living in cheap college rental housing, this was out of the question. Even now, many years later, the idea of making an athame (especially one with a steel blade) still seems impractical, and I'm not alone in that feeling.

In the course of researching this book, I asked many of my friends and acquaintances how they acquired their athames. The only folks who made their own athames were all blacksmiths or people who had crafted their knives while working hand in hand with one. Some of history's most famous Witches (like Janet and Stewart Farrar) have admitted in print to simply buying their blades.[15]

Constructing an athame from scratch sounds appealing, but for most of us it's just not possible. For anyone wanting to go that route, I suggest contacting a local metalsmith and asking if it might be possible to work with them directly. There are also outdoor Pagan festivals that sometimes bring in blacksmiths to work with individuals wishing to make their own blades. (For a list of Pagan festivals in your area, I suggest consulting The Witches' Voice website at witchvox.com.) Working with trained and experienced professionals just seems like a good idea to me when dealing with power tools and red-hot metal.

The easiest way to shop for an athame these days is online. Type *athame* into any Internet search engine and you'll come up with hundreds of hits. Online athames range in price from

15   Janet and Stewart Farrar, *A Witches' Bible*, p. 251.

just a couple of bucks to several hundred dollars. While it is true that you get what you pay for, a fifteen-dollar athame is just as serviceable as a two-hundred-dollar one.

Buying an athame online does come with its share of risks. Most online sellers won't tell you where the knives they are selling come from. Most of us, as a matter of necessity, are forced to buy things from Chinese sweatshops, but is that really where you want a magical tool to come from? I'm sure there are ritual tools on my altar of rather dubious origin, but I try to avoid such things when I can.

Many of the more decorative athames sold online also look sort of cheap. It might be cool to have a pentacle on the hilt of your athame's blade, but if that pentacle is made from plastic that's just going to fall off in a few months, I don't see the point. What matters most in an athame is functionality, not how well it's decorated. When buying an athame online, oftentimes simple is better.

The biggest problem with buying an athame online is that you can't hold it before you buy it. More than anything else, an athame should feel comfortable in your hands, and the only way to know if the "feel" is right is to hold it. If you do end up buying online, read reviews of the website and feedback from customers. If the online store has a good reputation, it's more likely that the blade feel will be a positive one.

Making an Athame Yours

While I'm wary of Internet athame purchases, my latest blade came from an online seller. In this case, the seller was an artisan who hand-made all of his knives. I got a great feeling after sending him some emails, and the moment I first saw his work, I felt an instant connection. He also had a good reputation among Witches online. I did my homework and it paid off. You can do the same.

There are lots of brick-and-mortar options when it comes to buying an athame. My first blade came from a local metaphysical store. Not all New Age/Pagan shops carry blades, but many do, and when buying an athame from a local retailer, you can get a better idea of how and where it was made. You can also usually pick up the blade and perhaps even swing it around a little bit.

For areas without a metaphysical shop, gun and knife stores are an alternative. Blades from such stores are often of high quality, and again it provides an opportunity to touch the blade and ask questions of the shop owner. I've never been to a gun and knife show, but I have friends who have had good luck finding an athame at such places. Many commercial shopping areas also have stores specializing in imported goods, and some of these stores sell decorative swords and knives. One of my friends bought a broadsword from such a place that he eventually gave to me.

My wife bought her current athame at a Pagan festival. Not every region has big Pagan gatherings, but many do. Oftentimes craftspeople who don't have a physical storefront attend such events and sell their wares. Such events provide a wonderful opportunity not only to look at blades but to meet the people who made them.

An athame does not have to be purchased new; if it speaks to you, a used blade is perfectly acceptable. Used blades can be found at secondhand and antique stores, as well as military surplus outlets. If you do purchase a used athame, feeling it out is of vital importance, because who knows what was done with it! If the energy is really bad, don't buy the blade; it's as simple as that. Also avoid any knife that has a large degree of negativity attached to it. It might seem cool to buy a Nazi knife from World War II, but that's exactly *not* the type of blade that belongs in a ritual circle.

The most important part of any athame purchase is that you feel good about it. You should feel good about where the blade came from, and the knife should feel good in your hand. In ritual, the athame is an extension of yourself; it should feel powerful, but it also should feel as if it belongs in your hand. Unless you are part of an established tradition, there's really no right or wrong about an athame. If it works for you, that makes it the right athame for you!

Making an Athame Yours

Creating the Black-Handled Knife

Many Wiccan traditions exclusively call for an athame with a black handle made from wood. When I joined one of those traditions, I thought that finding a black-handled knife would be easy, but sadly that's not the case. The wooden part of the hilt is generally easy enough to find, but the black part can be a bit more challenging.

Using a Wood Stain

The easiest way to turn a brown knife hilt black is to use a black wood stain. I'm not at all crafty but even I find this to be a pretty easy operation. Before staining the hilt, you'll want to do two things. First, protect the part of the knife that doesn't require stain. Wrap the knife's pommel and crossguard in an easy-to-remove tape; masking tape works especially well here. After that's completed, you'll want to do a bit of sanding on the knife's hilt. Your goal here is simply to remove whatever finish is already on the hilt. This shouldn't take all that long—just a couple of minutes.

After you're done sanding, apply the black wood stain. Since the surface area is pretty small, it's best to use a brush here, but some people swear by dabbing a bit of stain on a rag and then working that into the wood. Whatever you do, try to go with the grain of the wood if that's something you can detect. If it's not, simply apply the stain in whatever way feels right to you. Magically speaking, there are some who swear by a "bottom up" movement since it seems to imply "gain," but that's only necessary if such associations work for you personally.

After applying the initial coat of stain, you may decide that you need to add more. It just depends on how dark you want the handle. Also, stain doesn't work quite like paint; it's sometimes best to let your first coat of stain seep into the wood a bit before going further. Once the hilt is sufficiently dark, wipe off any excess stain with a rag. The last step is to apply a coat of wood finish to the hilt. That will protect the wood and give it a polished look. (You can also buy products that mix the stain and finish together.) Once everything is dry, you are good to go.

Using Fire to Turn a Hilt Black

A friend of mine once shared another trick with me for turning brown wood black, and this one involves fire. There's nothing wrong with simply staining a knife hilt, but the fire technique certainly feels witchier. This is not an immediate fix; it takes a few sessions, but it's worth the extra effort.

Start by sanding the hilt and removing the old wood finish. It's important to remove all of the finish, because such products are often petroleum-based and you really don't want to set your athame on fire. All you really need for the second part is a large taper candle with a longer-than-average wick (which you can "make" yourself simply by picking up the candle after it's lit and tipping it a bit). I think it's best to blacken the athame handle on a personal altar, but that's a personal preference.

Before starting, invite the gods to be a part of your work. The exact words you use aren't all that important; just ask them to watch over you and keep you safe. When that's done, carefully hold the blade and begin moving the hilt through the candle flame. If your blade is dull, you can simply hold on to the blade. If it's sharp, be sure to wear a glove during this part of the work. If wearing a glove feels a bit too mundane, you can wrap an altar cloth around the blade to protect your hand as well. Your goal is not to burn your athame but to scorch the hilt enough so that it turns black. This will take some time, and it's okay to do it over a series of days.

When the hilt reaches your desired level of darkness, apply a coat of wood stain to it. If you don't apply a bit of stain to it, all of the "black" will leave the knife and end up on your hands! An alternative method is to rub the hilt with beeswax until the hilt is smooth and it no longer smudges. Whatever method you choose (fire or stain) will produce the same result, and neither method is better than the other.

Making an Athame Your Own

Even if most of us will never be in a position to create our own steel athames from scratch, there are still several things we all can do to make a store-bought athame our own. One of the easiest and most effective ways to personalize an athame is by adding a personal mark to it. There are several magical alphabets that can be used for such marks, along with some symbols found exclusively in modern Witchcraft.

Marking an athame is an extremely personal decision and is not a requirement. Like a tattoo, most marks end up being permanent, so I advise caution. If you aren't completely comfortable with the Horned God, for instance, don't add his symbol to your blade. Adding a mark to your blade is a great cosmetic touch, but it will never be more important than actually using and getting in touch with the blade.

Marking the Athame

Many Witches choose to mark their athames with words and/or symbols. These marks can be left on either the hilt or the blade of the knife. There's no right or wrong when it comes to writing on an athame; it's simply a matter of personal preference. In his book *High Magic's Aid*, Gerald Gardner includes a picture of an athame containing both symbols and words, but not all Witches choose to mark their athames.

If you choose to mark your athame, you can use whatever symbols and alphabets you like, but some are more traditional than others. Personally I'm partial to traditional "Witch symbols," some of which were a part of *High Magic's Aid* (and before that the *Key of Solomon*). Those symbols don't cover every aspect of Witchcraft, but they do suggest a few of the bigger ideas within the practice. The seven symbols included here certainly aren't all the symbols that have been used by Witches over the years, but they do represent some of the more popular ones.

1. **The Spoked Wheel:** This represents the Wheel of the Year and the continual life, death, and rebirth of the natural world.

2. **The Horned God:** The Horned God is the ruler of the natural world and the most popular male deity in modern Witchcraft. This symbol is especially fitting for an athame, as the athame is usually considered a tool that contains male energy.

3. **Goddess of the Moon:** This symbol represents the Goddess as personified in the waxing and waning moon. The symbol on the left represents her as the new moon, and the symbol on the right as the full moon.

4. **Ankh:** The ankh is an ancient Egyptian symbol representing eternal life and the immortality of the soul.

5. **The Perfect Couple:** In many Witchcraft traditions, the polarities that create life are represented by the female and the male: the Goddess and the God. Together, the Lord and the Lady are thought to be the perfect couple, balancing out each other's strengths and weaknesses. This is a good symbol to use if you have a strong relationship with the Goddess and the God and like to

consistently honor them jointly during ritual. It's also a powerful symbol to use if you have a dedicated working partner (male or female) you feel especially close to. The perfect couple does not need to be male and female; it can be of one or two genders!

Spoked Wheel

Goddess of the Moon

Perfect Couple

Power Going Forth

Horned God

Ankh

Pentagram

Symbols to put on an athame

6. **The Pentagram:** The pentagram has many meanings. It has become a generic symbol for Witchcraft over the last several decades, and with its point upward is said to represent the triumph of the spiritual over the material. In Christianity, the pentagram was used to represent the five wounds of Jesus on the cross and serves as a symbol of self-sacrifice.

7. **The Power Going Forth:** This symbol looks like an arrow with a little Horned God symbol attached to the end of it. In some traditions it's considered a symbol of the Horned God and represents his sharing his power with the world. In other traditions it represents the power created by two polarities, most often expressed by the Goddess and the God, but not exclusively so.

Theban Script and the Norse Runes

Some Witches choose to write their names or other messages onto their athames. Some of them use the Latin alphabet we are all familiar with, but many more choose to use an exotic script or runic alphabet. Theban script is the most common Witch alphabet and has been in use since the sixteenth century. (See appendix 1 for a Theban alphabet.)

Theban script has many advantages over magical alphabets, the first one being that it's completely unique. Many other magical alphabets "look like something else," but Theban simply looks like Theban. Its symbols are not a part of any other writing system. Theban does lack both a *u* and a *w*, which is usually worked around by substituting the symbol for *v* in such instances.

People use magical alphabets because it calls for increased concentration. If you choose to mark your athame with a word spelled out in Theban, it's going to take some extra time and effort. All of that extra time, effort, and energy will then go into your blade, making it even more powerful.

The most common thing written on an athame is the name of the athame's owner. In many magical traditions, names are thought to have power, and it's believed that it's best never to reveal your "true name" to anyone you don't trust completely. For many Witches, their true name corresponds to their Witch or magical name. Writing that name on the blade in Theban keeps the name a secret to outsiders while conferring ownership and mastery over the athame.

Magical mottos are also things commonly written onto athames. A magical motto could be an idea adopted by a Witch or something related to their family or interests. The idea of the *magical motto* was first conceived by the nineteenth-century British group the Orthodox Order of the Golden Dawn. Upon entrance into the group, every initiate had to choose a motto that represented their inner self, and sometimes the motto even served as a magical name. Oftentimes the mottos were in Latin, but not exclusively. The English occultist Aleister Crowley, for example, chose the word *Perdurabo* ("I Will endure to the end") as his motto.

The second most popular alphabet in Witch circles is the Elder Futhark, most commonly referred to as "the runes." The Elder Futhark is the oldest and most common runic alphabet in existence, and its runes can be used as a substitute for the Latin alphabets or used to represent a single idea. Runes are especially useful for conveying an idea with a minimum of writing. (For a full list of the runes of the Elder Futhark and their correspondences, see appendix 2.)

If you choose to work with spirits, you may want to inscribe your athame with a rune of protection instead of spelling out the word *protection*. In that case, you'd draw the rune *eolh* on your athame. If you wanted to put a symbol for the element of fire on your athame, you'd use the rune *kenaz*, which is said to represent the hearth. I've never added a rune to my athame, but I use them often in spellwork.

Marking the Hilt

The easiest way to add a word or symbol to an athame is to mark the knife's handle. This can be done with a permanent marker or paint. The downside to using a marker is that it simply won't feel very magical and will most likely fade over time. Paint is a more permanent option but might also rub off.

Using a brush at least feels sort of magical, but that's never the case with a marker.

The most involved way to place a symbol on your athame's hilt is with a wood-burning pen. The advantage of a wood-burning pen is that the process will both feel magical and last a lifetime. The downside is if that you make a mistake, there's no going back; paint and ink can be washed away, but a scorch mark is forever. Wood-burning pens sound expensive but can be picked up for under twenty dollars. Many of them now come with a multitude of tips so you can make your symbols as wide or as narrow as you choose.

Etching the Blade

The most common mark on an athame is an etching burned directly into the blade. As when using a wood-burning tool on the handle, etching requires precision and patience on the part of the Witch. Make a mistake during the etching process and that mistake will live forever on your knife. Etching is a chemical process that "eats" away some of the metal. Alternatively, you can also *engrave* the blade of your knife, but that requires special tools beyond the reach of many Witches.

Etching can be done cheaply and easily with just a few materials. You'll need some sort of commercially available acid. The two most common types are ferric chloride acid and muriatic acid. Ferric chloride can be purchased at electronic stores, while muriatic acid is easily found at swimming-pool supply shops. You'll also need what's known as a *resist* to protect the parts of your blade you don't want etched. Many professionals recommend using nail polish, but I've known Witches who have used candle wax as a resist. If you use nail polish, you'll also want some nail polish remover. Conveniently, acetone is found in many nail polish removers and is also useful for cleaning steel, so even if you don't use nail polish for the etching, you'll still want some acetone.

Start by removing any oils on your blade by putting some acetone onto a rag and rubbing down your athame. When the blade is clean, apply the nail polish or wax. If you use nail polish, let it dry for a little bit, but begin "writing" on the blade while the polish is still tacky to the touch. The goal here is to remove the nail polish so the metal underneath can be etched by the acid. It's not extremely difficult to write on the nail polish, but it's not quite like writing on a piece of paper. If you make a mistake, simply apply more nail polish and start over again. I usually use a pin or a needle for this part of the process.

If you use wax, the instructions are basically the same, and again I recommend a needle or a pin for the writing. Anytime I light a candle, I feel witchy, and there's certainly something more magical about using a candle than a bottle of nail polish, but the wax will be more difficult to remove at the end of the process.

I would love to tell you that I chant magick words and infuse my etchings with magick while I'm working on them, but I'm usually far too focused on the task at hand to add anything to it. I do sometimes work on my altar (stripped of many of its more fragile belongings) and I might light some incense while working, but that's about as involved as I can get. My athames are very important to me, and I want to give them my full attention.

After you've scratched the words, symbols, or runes you want into the athame, simply dip it in a bowl of the acid. You have to be careful here, of course. You don't want to put the handle in the bowl; in fact, I suggest putting as little of the blade as possible directly in the acid. The chemical process of etching takes about an hour, but I recommend checking your blade every ten to fifteen minutes or so. When the blade has been etched to your satisfaction, take it out of the acid and then remove the nail polish with the acetone. When you're done removing the polish, you'll want to spiff up your blade with a metal polish to restore its former luster.

Wax is harder to remove than nail polish, but it's not an impossible task, just a time-consuming one. Your first step will be to put your athame in a freezer for a few hours. Wax comes off so easily when it's frozen and can often be removed in large chunks this way. Just carefully pry the frozen wax off your blade. I recommend using a dull butter knife. If this doesn't remove all the wax from your athame, you'll have to resort to more drastic measures, like boiling water! Place your athame in a large bowl, heat up some water, and then pour that water over the blade. While the wax is still melty, wipe it off of your athame with an old rag. Once the wax is all gone, polish up your blade and you're done!

To Be Sharp or Dull—A Difference of Opinion

Traditionally, knives are sharp; they're designed to be. It's hard to cut anything other than butter with a dull knife. However, there are many Witches who believe the athame should be kept dull. This is primarily a safety concern, since many Witches who work together do so in small spaces. The thinking here is that if a group of people are going to be continually raising, lowering, and swinging around their athames, it's safer to have a dull blade. We don't want anyone losing an ear!

Since the athame is rarely used for any physical cutting, a dull blade isn't much of an issue. Unless you are a Kitchen Witch who continually uses an athame in the kitchen, a blunt knife won't get in the way of any magical working. Even a candle can be carved with a blunt knifepoint.

Not everyone agrees with having a dull blade though. There are also a lot of Witches out there who believe that a blade should be sharp. By its very nature, a knife is designed to be sharp, so having a dull one implies that it's not being used to its maximum potential. The athame is also an extension of the individual Witch's energy and will, and a sharp blade is all the better for projecting those forces. They believe that their focus should match their athames, and that both should always be sharp.

I've met people who continually sharpen their blades, and their athames are nearly sharp enough to cut a strand of hair. I also know people who have taken great pains to dull their blades. I've always worked between the two extremes. The blade of my athame isn't dull, but I wouldn't characterize it as sharp either. However, I do keep the point of my blade sharp. The tip of my knife is where the energy is released, so I want it as focused as possible.

Having a sharp or a dull blade is ultimately a personal decision. If you think a sharp blade in the circle is a safety issue, then by all means dull your blade. If you believe that a dull knife makes for a dull mind, then keep your athame sharp. How we perceive our ritual tools has a lot to do with their effectiveness. If you believe your tool is less than optimal, it will operate in such a way. If you work with a coven that requires a dull blade and you prefer a sharp one, get a second athame and follow the instructions of the coven during group rituals and then follow your own instincts away from that circle.

Care and Keeping of Your Athame

Magical tools should be treated with care and respect, and the athame is no exception to that rule. Athames don't require a high degree of maintenance, but there are several things you can do on a yearly basis to keep them in optimal condition. If you love your blade and truly feel that it's an extension of your will, you'll want to do everything possible to keep it in good repair.

The biggest problem steel blades have is rust. Even stainless steel will rust, but you can minimize the chances of that happening with an application of oil. A light coating of oil applied two or three times a year creates a barrier between the blade and the air. It's especially important in humid and coastal areas to apply a bit of blade oil. Not only is the water bad for your athame, but so is the salt in the air!

There are several different brands of oil on the market specifically for knives, but most types of household oil work well. Something as common as vegetable oil can be used on your athame's blade, but it will break down quickly. If you choose to protect your blade with something like canola oil, you will have to reapply it once every two weeks. If your blade is going to come into contact with food or drink, be sure to avoid most petroleum oils. Food-grade mineral oil is fine, but even something like petroleum jelly can make a person sick.

Keeping your athame dry is a rather obvious suggestion but one that many people in the circle miss. I use my athame during the rite of cakes and ale and to cleanse and consecrate water at the beginning of ritual. These are both acts that bring my athame into direct contact with liquids. After getting my blade wet, I tend to immediately wipe it on a leg of my pants. If I'm doing ritual skyclad, I casually wipe the blade off on the altar cloth. I'm usually capable of doing this without anyone noticing. My wife does the same after she cleanses salt with her athame during our rituals.

One thing that you don't want to do is store your athame in a leather sheath. Many knives come with leather sheaths, but those sheaths should be used sparingly. If everyone in your coven uses an athame during ritual and there's not enough room to store them all on the altar, keeping them sheathed and on the person of each individual member is a great idea. This is the perfect situation for using a leather sheath that can be clipped onto a belt or belt loop. However, once the ritual is over, you'll want to get your athame out of its leather cage.

Leather contains several acids that can corrode a steel blade, and the longer you leave your blade in contact with those acids, the easier it will be for them to damage your athame. When I'm not using my athame, I usually leave it on our ritual altar unsheathed. (I will admit that while writing this book I've kept it on my writing desk, but these are extraordinary circumstances.) If you are a Witch who prefers to keep your athame sheathed, find or make a sheath from synthetic materials or cloth. Nylon, which is moisture-resistant, is a very good material from which to make a sheath.

A simple sheath can be made with just a few materials. Start by tracing your knife blade on a piece of paper. Then make a mirror image of that tracing a quarter of an inch larger than the original one. (You want your sheath to be slightly larger than your blade.) Cut out the larger quarter-inch version and you've got the pattern for your sheath.

Fold in half whatever material you are using for the sheath, and place your pattern on top of that. I usually use pencil here to trace the pattern onto the material, but if you want to be really fancy you can use tailor's chalk. Now carefully cut out the material you'll use for your sheath, being careful to stay within the lines you've drawn. When you are done, you should have two pieces of fabric.

The tracing and cutting is the easy part. The hard part is getting the two pieces of your sheath to stay together. There are some easy ways out here. A light coating of fabric glue around the edges will do the trick, at least for a while. (It's doubtful the glue will hold for very long.) Stitching is always the best solution here, but it can be hard to keep the two pieces of material together during the process. This can be overcome with the use of some bias tape placed around the edges of the sheath. Bias tape is made to bend, so it should easily loop around the edges of your material. The last step is simply to sew around the edges, and voilà! You have a mostly functional knife sheath!

If you want a more elaborate sheath, you can decorate the material before stitching the two pieces together. You might want to add a symbol of protection, for instance. If you are using an especially tough and rigid material (like nylon), you might also want to include a belt loop. You'll want to sew or glue the belt loop onto the material you are using before stitching it onto its partner.

If you have a leather sheath and don't want to bother with making another sheath, you can also wrap your blade in a thin cloth before placing it back in the sheath. This will keep the leather acids away from your athame while keeping the blade "locked up." It's also possible to add a layer of material to a leather sheath to keep steel and leather from touching.

Acetone is a readily available cleaner that will help keep your blade in top shape. Fingerprints (with their natural human oils) are also an enemy of stainless steel, and a rag with a bit of acetone will remove those quickly. Be sure to keep the cleaner from touching your knife's hilt; what's good for metal may not be good for wood, bone, or plastic.

If your athame does develop a little rust, there are several easy ways to get rid of it. You can remove rust from a clean blade by soaking the steel in white vinegar for a couple of hours. If you can't figure out a way to keep the vinegar from touching your knife's hilt, simply soak a rag in the vinegar and then wrap that around the blade. White vinegar takes only a few hours to have an effect, so after about four hours, remove the blade from the vinegar and wipe it down. The rust should come off pretty easily. When you are done, oil the blade.

If you don't have any vinegar around, there are several other common household items that can be used to remove rust with almost equal effectiveness. You can spray some WD-40 onto your blade and then wipe it off in a few hours; this will often remove any light rust. Petroleum jelly also works well. One of my favorite ways to remove rust from metal is with ketchup. I had an old corroded bell that I stuck in a bowl of ketchup for twenty-four hours. After I removed it from the ketchup, it looked brand-new.

Potatoes are a fun way to remove rust too. Simply stick the rusty part of your athame into a potato. The oxalic acid in the potato will get rid of the rust. Onions work in a similar way, but potatoes don't make me cry! After using whatever methods you choose, wipe the blade off and then oil it up to protect it in the future.

If you keep your blade dry and well oiled, it should last a lifetime or more! I know people who have inherited their knives from deceased brothers and sisters in the Craft, and those knives sometimes still look new fifty or sixty years later. Treat your athame well and it will do the same for you in your magical workings.

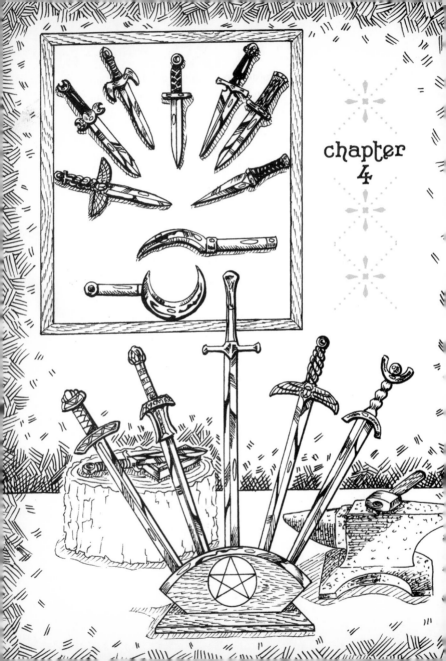

chapter
4

Preparing the Athame for Ritual

Before being used for ritual, the athame should be cleansed and consecrated. Cleansing the blade isn't a physical washing but a spiritual one. It's done to remove any lingering psychic residue that might possibly be on the blade from a previous owner or even the knife's manufacturer. To consecrate an athame is to dedicate the blade to your ritual practice and the gods you serve. Many times "cleansing" the blade isn't necessary, but consecrating always is.

Cleansing an Athame: Outdoor Method

If you bought your athame used or it was given to you as a gift, you may want to cleanse the blade. I've had friends who have received used blades and sometimes they prefer to keep a little of the original owner's energy in their knife, but that isn't always the case. If the previous owner of the knife is unknown to you or your athame just doesn't feel right while holding it, I suggest cleansing the blade before taking it into ritual space.

The easiest way to cleanse a blade and remove any old energies attached to it is to dig a hole in your backyard and bury the blade for about a month. Let Mother Earth take away any negative energies lingering in your athame! If you do decide to bury your blade, it's best to bury it on a night of the full moon. As the moon wanes from full moon to new, the negative energies that are in the knife will seep into the ground and away from your blade. If the ground in your area is excessively moist, wrap your athame in a small piece of canvas to protect it. Barring that, a piece of plastic will work too, though I'd put a small hole or two in it to allow the energy from the knife to dissipate into the ground.

There's no need for an extensive ceremony when burying your athame, but a few words stating your intent would be a good idea. I usually dig my hole and set the tool I'm cleansing into it. Then I say:

Great Goddess, Mistress of the Moon and Mother of us all, into your womb I place this blade. Take away from it all impurities and negative energies so that it might be a valuable tool to use in service to you and your consort. So mote it be!

While filling the hole and burying my athame, I usually say a few words with each scoop of dirt I throw over it, such as *Earth, cleanse my blade!* or *Be gone into the ground, My blade now safe and sound!*

When I've finished burying my blade, I mark the spot and then leave a gift to the earth on that spot. A coin would work, but I think the earth would most likely prefer a big drink of water.

Two weeks later, on a night of the new moon, return to where you buried your athame and dig back to the spot where it's resting in the earth. Now place something in tune with your own energies (such as another working tool, an item you have an attachment to, or even just a rock that you've charged) next to your athame so that the blade starts to feel comfortable with you. Again, it's best to speak your intent while going through this next step:

Lady Mother, Great Goddess, hear my prayer as I place this (name of item) next to my athame. May my blade learn to recognize me and my energies so that I might use it in service to you and your consort. So mote it be!

After stating your intent, rebury your athame and the additional item together, making sure that they are touching each other. If you are wrapping your athame in anything, be sure to rewrap it and the extra item.

On the night of the next full moon, dig up your athame and, under the light of the full moon, take a moment to feel its energies. If your athame still doesn't feel right, leave it in the ground for another month. Most likely, though, your blade will be cleansed of any negativity and will be ready for consecration. After you've refilled the hole where your blade was buried, look up at the moon and drive the blade of your athame into the earth while saying:

Great Goddess, Mistress of the Moon and Mother of us all, you have heard my prayers and cleansed this blade. I give my thanks to the earth and to the Lord and the Lady for helping me to prepare this blade! Blessed be!

This process can be repeated with any tool that needs special cleansing.

Cleansing an Athame: Indoor Method

If you don't have access to a backyard or are unable to dig a hole, there's a slightly less involved way to cleanse an athame entirely indoors. I call this the "altar method," and it is generally what I use to prepare all of my ritual tools. For most Witches, the altar is where they store their magical tools and do most of their work. Because of that, it's a very "charged" space and is generally filled with the essence of the Witch who works there.

When a Witch doesn't have a permanent working altar, there are other options. For some of us, the top of our dresser where all of our "stuff" accumulates works well as a makeshift altar. The top of a bookshelf or coffee table is another option, and if your life revolves around your kitchen, a spot in there works well too. The important thing is that whatever space you use should be filled with your own energies.

Ideally the blade should be placed on the altar (or other space) on a night of the full moon, but if you can't wait that long, that's okay too. I usually build a "nest" around my athame out of silk cloth before setting it down on my altar. Part of this is presentation; as a new addition to my magical arsenal, it seems fitting that my athame should come wrapped in swaddling clothes. And part of this is for practical reasons that we'll get to soon. After setting down your athame, speak your intent:

Great Goddess, Mistress of the Moon and Mother of us all, on my altar I place this blade. Take away from it all impurities and negative energies so that it might be a valuable tool to use in service to you and your consort. So mote it be!

Now take some salt (sea salt is best, but even good old iodized table salt works) and sprinkle it on the blade while saying:

With the power of the earth and the sacred salt, I remove from this athame all negativity so that it might do good in my practice. So mote it be!

Once a week and for a full moon cycle, repeat the sprinkling of salt on your blade. Salt is one of the best cleansing items available to the Witch and has all sorts of practical applications.

The salt will remove anything negative from your blade, and putting the blade in your place of power will get it in tune with your personal energies. There's no better place to help a new tool find "you." After a month on your altar (or longer or shorter, depending on your personal preference), take the athame in your hands and thank the gods for cleansing it:

Great Goddess, Mistress of the Moon and Mother of us all, you have heard my prayers and cleansed this blade. I give my thanks to the Lord and the Lady for helping me to prepare this blade. Blessed be!

Now your athame is ready to be consecrated.

The Whys and Whats of Consecrating

Consecrating an item serves many functions. First of all, it's a declaration that whatever you are consecrating is special and being singled out for a specific purpose—in our case, for Witchcraft. Consecrating an item is a way of declaring to the world and the gods that your tool is sacred and holy and worthy to be used in rites praising the Lord and the Lady.

Consecration also bonds an item to you (or, in some cases, the coven). Consecrating your athame is a way of saying, *This object is* mine *and is in some ways an extension of me.* The consecration of the athame prepares it for your use and helps to create a bond with it. Your athame should not just feel good in your hand, it should feel like a part of you, when all is said and done.

Finally, consecrating a tool makes it sacred to the gods you serve and honor. As a Witch, I worship the Horned God and the Great Lady, and when I consecrate my ritual tools, I ask for their blessings so that I might do their will with my ritual tools. My gods would never ask me to give up my sense of self for them, but I feel as if what I do as a Witch is influenced by them and I often ask them to guide my hand.

A Solitary Consecration Rite

Before starting, be sure to prepare your altar with representatives of all four elements. I usually use a dish of sea salt (earth), incense (air), a candle flame (fire), and a dish of water. To represent the Lord and the Lady, I generally use deity statues, but you can also use other objects to represent them, such as a seashell for the Goddess or a piece of horn or antler for the God. If those are unavailable, they can be represented by candles. Ask for the blessings of the gods over all of your items before starting the consecration rite.

Begin ritual as is customary to you (calling quarters, casting a circle, etc.—directions for both are in this book; however, they do require a consecrated athame—oh, the catch-22!). Once the gods have been invoked, begin the consecration rite. Start in the east and let the incense smoke surround your blade. Slowly and gently cut into the smoke and imagine the incense cleaning any psychic impurities from your blade while saying:

With the power of air, I bless and consecrate this athame that it may serve me in my rites and always honor the Lord and the Lady! By the spirits of the east, this blade has now received the favor of air. So mote it be!

Move to the south and move the blade of your athame through the candle flame on your altar. As the blade is cleansed and purified with flame, say these words:

With the power of fire, I bless and consecrate this athame that it may serve me in my rites and always honor the Lord and the Lady! By the spirits of the south, this blade has now received the favor of fire. So mote it be!

If you are using a bowl or chalice that is large enough to dip your athame into, do so now. If you aren't using a vessel that large, simply cup a little water in your power hand (the one you predominantly use) and sprinkle it over the blade. As the water covers or drips onto the steel, see it washing the blade and bathing it in the powers of the west. Now ask for the blessings of water for your athame:

With the power of water, I bless and consecrate this athame that it may serve me in my rites and always honor the Lord and the Lady! By the spirits of the west, this blade has now received the favor of water. So mote it be!

Salt can be used in a way similar to water. If your bowl of salt is large, set your blade into it. If your vessel for earth is small, simply sprinkle some cleansing salt along the blade while saying:

With the power of earth, I bless and consecrate this athame that it may serve me in my rites and always honor the Lord

Preparing the Athame for Ritual

and the Lady! By the spirits of the north, this blade has now received the favor of earth. So mote it be!

Once the athame has been blessed by all four elements, it's time to ask for the blessings of the gods upon it. Hold your athame and place the flat of your blade near the Goddess statue or the object representing her on your altar. (If you are using a candle, place the blade in the candle flame.) As you hold the athame there, close your eyes and picture the Goddess standing behind you. Feel her touch on your arm as you hold your blade and then ask for her blessings upon it:

Great Goddess, Eternal Lady, I ask that you bless and consecrate this athame for my use and your greater glory. May it only be used for acts of love and beauty and in service to the Witches' Craft. In the name of the Lady, so mote it be!

Now touch the blade to your statue or representation of the God. Close your eyes and feel his power fill the room. When you feel him near you and guiding your hand, say these words:

Horned One, Great Lord, I ask that you bless and consecrate this athame for my use and your greater glory. May it serve me in all of my magical endeavors and protect me from all harm in the magick circle. In the name of the Horned One, so mote it be!

Your athame is now consecrated and ready to use in ritual. In some traditions, however, consecration is only the beginning! Some Witches believe that the newly consecrated athame should be kept in physical contact with its owner for up to a month. Others call for at least sleeping with it (carefully) under a pillow for several weeks. I do believe that if you can, you should touch it and use it as much as possible in the days after its consecration. The more you use it, the better it will work for you in circle.

A Coven Consecration Rite

If you practice with a coven or have a working partner, here's an alternative consecration ritual. I actually prefer to consecrate my tools privately and then present them and consecrate them a second time in a coven/group setting, but this double dipping is not necessary. This particular rite calls for only two people, but with a little creativity, the parts can be split up to bring more people into the ritual.

Whoever you perform this ritual with should be someone you hold "in perfect love and perfect trust." Not only will they be helping you to consecrate your blade, they will also be handling the blade for large parts of the ritual. If the person helping you with the rite has their own athame or sword, they should place it upon the altar at the start of ritual with your athame lying on top of, and touching, it. As for the solitary rite just described, be sure to have water, salt, incense, and fire available to represent the four elements.

Begin the ritual as your coven normally does, calling the quarters, casting the circle, etc. After the gods have been invoked, pick up your athame and hold it above your head. Address the coven and tell them your desires, then present the athame to your coven's high priestess/priest or whoever is helping you with your ritual:

> *I come here tonight seeking your blessings and assistance in consecrating this athame. Will you lend your light and love to me in this task?*

The high priestess should pick up the blade and nod, saying:

> *Yes, we will help you with this task. Now stand beside me and place your hand upon the athame with mine.*

Now stand beside the priestess and join with her as she consecrates the blade. You can say the words provided here together, or repeat them after her.

> *Through smoke and flame, we bless this blade. Through air and fire, we consecrate thee, O blade, so that ye might serve (your*

name or magical name) in beauty and strength upon the magical path of the Witch!

Slowly drag the athame through first the incense smoke and then the candle flame. Be sure to flip the blade over so both sides of it are exposed to the air and fire.

Still holding the blade, together place one measure of salt into the bowl of water upon the altar and mix them together. (If you already have some salted water on your altar, you can just use that.) Once the two elements are mixed, set your athame down on a pentacle (if available). You and the priestess should be touching the athame with your non-dominant hands. With your power hand, sprinkle some salted water on the blade and hilt while saying:

Through rain and salt, we bless this blade. Through water and earth, we consecrate thee, O blade, so that ye might serve (your name or magical name) in beauty and strength upon the magical path of the Witch!

The high priestess should now touch the tip of your blade to her own, speaking these words:

Point to point, tip to tip, I now pass on a spark from my blade to yours. From the first gods to the first Witch, I consecrate this athame that it might be powerful in the circle and serve our sister (or brother) well.

101
• • •

With the high priestess, hold on to the hilt of the athame and ask for the blessings of the gods for your blade. Place the blade upon a statue or representation of the Goddess and recite these words separately or together:

In your presence and alongside my working partners in this coven, I seek your blessings for this athame, O Gracious Goddess! May this blade ever draw me closer to your ways. May it only be used for acts of love and beauty and in service to the Witches' Craft. So mote it be!

Now the two of you should hold your blade against the God statue upon the altar. These words can again be said by only one of you or together in unison:

In your presence and alongside my working partners in this coven, I seek your blessings for this athame, O Great Horned One! May this blade draw me closer to your mysteries. May it serve in all of my magical endeavors and protect me from all harm in the magick circle. So mote it be!

Let go of the blade and stand before the altar, leaving enough room for the high priestess to perform this version of the fivefold kiss in front of you. After saying each line, she should place the athame upon your body and then kiss the blade.

May you ever walk forward in the path of the wise.
(Athame is placed on the top of each foot and is then kissed.)

May you ever be free to kneel at the sacred altar.
(Athame is placed on each knee and is then kissed.)

May you ever love and be loved.
(Athame is placed upon the genitalia and is then kissed.)

May your heart ever beat in courage and strength.
(Athame is placed on the heart or between the breasts and is then kissed.)

May the names of the Lord and the Lady ever be upon your lips.
(The blade should be held straight upon your lips, with the high priestess then kissing you and the blade simultaneously.)

After the fivefold kiss is enacted, the high priestess should present you with your athame once more, saying:

By the power of the gods, the four elements, and this coven, your blade is now consecrated and ready to serve in the ways of the Witch. So mote it be!

The athame is now consecrated and ready for use.

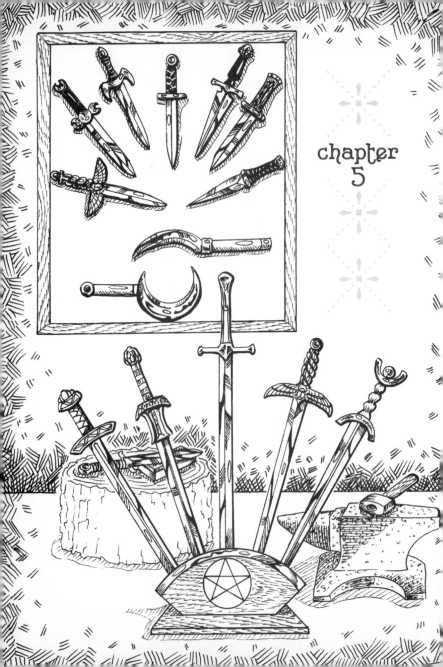

The Athame in Ritual

As a ritual tool, the athame stands alone. It is the only personal tool every member of the coven is encouraged to bring with them to ritual, and it's the only tool used in a wide variety of ritual practices. Because of its great importance to the individual Witch, it's sometimes referred to as *first forged*. For many Witches the athame is *the* essential tool. It's the foundation of nearly of all ritual practice. Without the athame, there is no properly cast circle, no salute to the watchtowers, and no proper blessing of the cakes and ale.

The athame is more than just an active working tool; it's also a symbolic tool. It represents the male sphere of the great mystery, the Horned God, and often the phallus during the symbolic Great Rite. Only the chalice (or cup) is also used both symbolically and actively during ritual, and even then it's used much less than the athame. At this point in my life, I can't even imagine proper Witch ritual without an athame.

The Opening Ceremony

Before casting a circle and officially beginning ritual, my coven ritually blesses and consecrates the four elements of earth, air, fire, and water. The athame is central to this act, and both ritual leaders use their own blades during this portion of the ritual. Most Witches keep four active representations of the four elements on their altars during ritual. My coven uses salt (earth), a candle flame (fire), incense (air), and a shallow dish full of water (water).

Consecrating and preparing the elements is done to remove any negativity or unwanted energy in them before ritual. Unlike a broom or chalice, the salt, water, incense, and flame differ every time you use those elements in ritual. It's best to make sure there are no lingering presences left within them before the ritual starts. After preparing the elements, we use them to cleanse our ritual space and the coven.

In our circle, the act is begun by the high priest, who places his athame in a bowl, dish, or chalice of water while saying:

I consecrate thee, O element of water, and remove from thee all darkness and corruption. In thee now only light and goodness remain. In the names of the Lord and the Lady, so mote it be!

The words of the high priest describe what is going on as he places his athame in the water, but they aren't the essential part of the ritual.

What's truly important is visualizing the process of cleansing the water. Connect to the earth below your feet and feel its power rushing up through you. Then push that energy out through your athame. While projecting power into the water, picture that energy in the water, destroying anything negative within it. I see the energy as a sparkling blue electric light zapping anything unwanted in the water.

The element of earth is prepared next. In our circle, this is generally done by our high priestess, who takes her athame and places it in the dish of salt while saying:

I consecrate thee, O element of earth, and remove from thee all darkness and corruption. In thee now only light and goodness remain. In the names of the Lord and the Lady, so mote it be.

The cleansing process is identical to that of the water, with energy moving out from the athame and cleansing the salt.

The high priestess then removes three measures of salt and places them in the consecrated water. While placing the salt into the water, she says:

Thrice measured, thrice taken, thrice given. So mote it be!

Salt on the flat
of a blade

The high priestess then uses her athame to mix the salt with the water, picturing the two merging and becoming one in her mind's eye while doing so. Now properly prepared, the salted water is sprinkled around the ritual area and on the rite's participants.

I use salted water for all sorts of things magically. Anytime the energy in a room feels negative, I mix some up and sprinkle it around the room's perimeter, paying special attention to the corners. Salt is a magical powerhouse and is great for getting rid of things. Quietly drizzling some salted water near some unwanted guests is a great way to get rid of them.

Casting the Circle

The act most associated with the athame (and often sword; see chapter 8) is the act of casting the circle. The circle is where the Witch works her magick and communes with her gods. It's sacred space, and a place between the worlds where humans are free to mingle with the gods and other powerful forces. The circle keeps out negative forces and entities while serving as a holding space for positive energy.

A well-cast circle can make or break a ritual. I've been in circles that canceled out the mundane world so effectively that cellphones ceased to work inside of them. (I think it speaks volumes when a phone starts ringing the moment a circle is released.) Temperatures have a tendency to rise when in the circle; somehow the energies used in its creation act as a giant magical blanket. If you are working on raising energy for spell-work, a circle capable of containing that energy is a must. A spell is always going to be more effective when its energies are released in one great cosmic whoosh instead of having those energies trickle out slowly.

In most traditions, circle casting begins in the east, with the circle-caster walking deosil (clockwise) around the circle (though in the Southern Hemisphere circles are generally cast "sunwise," which is counterclockwise there). Circles are cast clockwise because that matches the order in which the elements are called and because clockwise is generally thought of as a direction of increase or abundance. Like time, the circle should move forward. I generally cast my circle three times for a little extra added oomph and protection.

The sword is often used for casting circles, but circumstances often make the sword an unwieldy and impractical choice in some groups. Swords are just generally more expensive than knives, and if ritual is being performed in a small space, it might be dangerous to use a sword. I've cast circles with both swords and athames over the years, and there's never been a lot of difference between the two.

A circle is created by projecting energy, and the athame serves as a focal point for that energy. I think of the energy I use to cast a circle as coming from two places. The first is from deep within the earth, and I can feel it coming up from the ground into my feet and then through the rest of my body. Energy also comes from inside the self. We all have deep wells of energy and power within ourselves; this is another source of energy that can be tapped while casting the circle.

We call them "circles," but a well-cast circle is more like a well-cast sphere. The energies of the circle aren't located simply at the perimeter of the room; they are above and below as well. When casting the circle, make sure to remember this and to project energy into all of the appropriate spaces.

Starting in the east, walk deosil around the circle projecting energy. I usually begin with my athame raised over my head and hold it there while making my first pass around the circle. On my second trip around I hold the athame level, and on the third pass I point it toward the ground. This way I feel like I've directed energy into all of the right spots in order to create my ritual "sphere." While casting the circle, I like to say the following words:

With athame in hand I now cast this circle thrice round. First pass to stand between the worlds and create sacred ground. Second pass to protect and keep all within safe from harm. Third pass to hold in our energies, magick, and charm. Consecrated in the names of the Lord and the Lady, the circle is now cast. So mote it be!

Witch casting circle with athame

People often make too big a deal out of the words while performing ritual. What's even more important than the words is the intent. If you don't feel the energy being used to create the circle, no number of fancy words will make up for that.

Once the circle has been cast, move around it only in a clockwise direction. Nothing catastrophic will happen if someone walks widdershins (counterclockwise), but the energies of the circle will flow more smoothly if everyone moves the same way within its borders. It's always easier to go with the flow of a river than attempting to swim upstream.

If anyone has to leave the circle during ritual, it's best to cut a doorway in the circle so as not to disrupt the circle's energy. If I'm outside, I usually create my doorway where I initially began the circle-casting process in the east. If I'm inside, I create the doorway near the most convenient way out of the ritual's location.

To create a doorway, take a deep breath and feel energy move up through you and into the athame. I usually create my doorways in the shape of a pyramid, starting to my left and cutting upward, then moving to my right on the down stroke. Visualize the energy of the circle remaining strong, with the doorway looking sort of like a scar on its surface. When cutting the doorway, it sometimes feels like I'm cutting magical threads.

When the person using the doorway has slipped through it, be sure to reseal it to retain the energy being raised in the circle. Re-knit the circle's threads by starting where you ended the doorway, moving back up to the triangle's point and then back down. Visualize the door closing and the circle healing, returning to how it was before you created the door.

At the end of ritual, it's important to "take down" the circle and make all as it once was. When closing down a ritual, I go in reverse order from how I started the ritual. That means taking down the circle tends to be the last major component of my rituals, followed only by a goodbye to my fellow coveners. If I cast the circle before calling the quarters, I will dismiss those quarters before taking it down.

To "uncast" the circle, start again in the east, but this time move widdershins around the circle. I start with my athame held low and visualize two things during the process. First, I visualize the energy used to create the circle returning to my athame. During this process I sometimes feel like a conduit; any energy taken from the earth during the circle casting is then returned there. This is also a good little trick for storing a bit of extra magick in your athame. Second, I envision the threads of the circle being cut.

As with the initial circle casting, I take three passes around the circle, finishing like I started, with my athame held high. Be sure to remember that the circle is a sphere; it's just as important to release the energy at the top and bottom of the sphere as it is to release the energy in the middle. While un-creating my circle, I recite the following words:

With athame in hand I now undo this circle round. First pass to return the sacred to mundane ground. Second pass to release all that kept us safe from harm. Third pass to release our spells, magick, and charm. In the names of the Lord and the Lady, all has been dismissed and all is now as it once was. The circle is open but never truly broken. So mote it be!

After taking down the circle, I like to ceremonially place my athame on the altar as a sign that the work is done.

Calling the Quarters

Inviting the elements of air, fire, water, and earth to ritual has a long tradition in the rituals of the Witch. People have been inviting the elements to guard and look over their rituals for hundreds of years. In many traditions calling the elements with the athame has become passé, but it remains a powerful and effective way to perform ritual.

Why use the athame when calling the quarters? The athame provides a strong focal point as the Witch attempts to bring the power of the elements into the circle. Think of the athame as a lightning rod. It's possible to attract the elements without an athame, but there's more control over where that energy lands when using a ritual blade.

When using the athame to call the quarters, my coven begins in the east with arms in the Osiris position. The Osiris position is similar to how a mummy is usually depicted lying in its sarcophagus or a vampire in its coffin. The arms are crossed in an *X* on the upper chest, dominant hand holding the athame on top.

From Osiris, move toward the east and salute that direction with your athame raised in the air and your non-dominant arm at your side. Now open yourself up to the power of air, feeling it enter the circle through the point of the athame. While the energy comes cascading down into the circle, "call" the quarter in the style you are most comfortable with. In my circle we use the following:

> *Spirits of the east, element of air and wind, powers of clear will and knowledge, we summon you to join us in our sacred circle. Guard, protect, and bless our joyous rite! Hail and welcome!*

After calling the quarter, draw an invoking pentagram in the air with the athame. Visualize energy coming from the athame creating a five-pointed star in the air. The invoking pentagram attracts a little more energy into the circle and puts a nice "bow" on the quarter-calling operation. Once the pentagram has been drawn, take the athame and place it upon your lips, kissing the blade. I often think of this as "blowing a kiss" to the elements, since when I use my fingers in place of an athame, it's very similar to how I blew kisses as a child. Then raise the athame once more in the air to salute and honor the elemental energy now in your circle.

Osiris position, to raised arm, and back to Osiris

117

Move your arms back into the Osiris position and pivot clockwise to the south. Then repeat the process for the element of fire:

Spirits of the south, element of fire and sun, powers of illumination and desire, we summon you to join us in our sacred circle. Guard, protect, and bless our joyous rite! Hail and welcome!

Draw the invoking pentagram once more, blow a kiss to the element of fire, resume the Osiris position, and smoothly pivot to face the west.

Once in the west again, salute with the athame while saying:

Spirits of the west, element of water and rain, powers of death and initiation, we summon you to join us in our sacred circle. Guard, protect, and bless our joyous rite! Hail and welcome!

The pentagram is drawn again and another kiss is blown. Arms move once more to Osiris, and the coven then faces the north.

Salute the element of earth while saying:

Spirits of the north, element of earth and field, powers of harvest and home, we summon you to join us in our sacred circle. Guard, protect, and bless our joyous rite! Hail and welcome!

A final pentagram is drawn in the north and another kiss is blown. Arms move once more to the Osiris position, and everyone in the circle then spins back to face the altar in the center of the ritual space.

Invoking pentagram

Many covens recite the quarter calls together in unison, while others simply appoint one quarter-caller for each of the four directions. In my coven we generally do not say the calls in unison, but every group should do what works for them. It is very traditional for each covener to draw the invoking (and later banishing) pentagrams at the conclusion of the quarter call. If space is an issue, it's fine to drop that particular tradition.

The Athame in Ritual

When I first began calling the quarters in this fashion, my first thought was, *Why the kiss?* The kiss to the elements is a show of respect. The elements have real power, and blowing them a kiss is a way to say thanks and to show that you respect that power. Think about how destructive fire, earth, water, and air can be! Those are energies you want on your side.

Many covens and circles light candles to represent the elements at the four quarters. I fell out of this practice years ago. When indoors, I often light quarter candles before the ritual begins, or light them in a separate ceremony performed before calling the elements. In my coven we call that bit of ritual "lighting the temple." When I'm outside, I don't even bother with quarter candles since the wind is likely to snuff them out pretty quickly.

Dismissing the energies gathered at the four quarters is an essential part of ritual. It might seem like a good idea to keep fire around on a cold winter's night, but it won't be such a good idea once dinner catches fire on the stove! The energies of Witchcraft are very real, and ceremonially dismissing them is a way to show respect toward that power.

To dismiss the quarters, start in the north and then move in a widdershins direction (north, west, south, and east). When turning toward the north, begin in the Osiris position before raising arm and athame. Visualize the energies of the four elements leaving the circle. If there's an abundance of that energy inside of yourself or the circle, it may move through you and then out via the athame. Moving the energy out via the athame keeps a little bit of it in the ritual blade, keeping it charged up for when it's used next. Drawing a banishing pentagram in the air with the athame helps to push the energies out of your ritual space and circle. While dismissing the quarters, I recite the following words:

Spirits of the north, element of earth and field, powers of harvest and home, we summoned you to guard, protect, and bless our rites. You have served us well, and now we wish you hail and farewell!

Spirits of the west, element of water and rain, powers of death and initiation, we summoned you to guard, protect, and bless our rites. You have served us well, and now we wish you hail and farewell!

Spirits of the south, element of fire and sun, powers of illumination and desire, we summoned you to guard, protect, and bless our rites. You have served us well, and now we wish you hail and farewell!

Spirits of the east, element of air and wind, powers of clear will and knowledge, we summoned you to guard, protect, and bless our rites. You have served us well, and now we wish you hail and farewell!

The Athame in Ritual

Banishing pentagram

While dismissing the quarters, I enact the same motions as I did when calling them, moving from the Osiris position to raised arms and back again. At the end of every dismissal is where I add the banishing pentagram. After drawing the pentagram, we again salute the quarters with a kiss to the blade. When dismissing an energy or entity from my circle, I also try to make sure to compliment them too. Everyone (and everything) likes to hear that they've done a good job.

One of the most imaginative uses for the athame I've ever seen in ritual came from my friend Dwayne. Instead of speaking when he dismissed the quarters, he simply walked up to them and snuffed out the candles used to represent them with his athame. It was a powerful way to end ritual, but it does get wax all over your blade!

The Symbolic Great Rite & Cakes and Ale

In many Wiccan traditions, the athame is seen as a symbolic representation of the phallus. It's not quite phallus-shaped, but as a tool designed somewhat for poking it's easy to see where the attribution originated. In Wicca, the athame as phallus represents one half of the magick needed to create new life. Many Wiccan traditions celebrate the polarity of male and female energies and symbolically represent those energies in the athame and the chalice. The chalice as representative of the womb is especially symbolic. Within the chalice lies the waters of life, and even now we humans are basically formed in a sac full of water.

The Great Rite originally referred to the act of sexual union, though the high priestess and high priest never performed it in front of others. These days, the Great Rite is usually expressed symbolically by the union of knife and cup. Some Witches find the practice far too heteronormative and believe that it implies that the gods are exclusively straight or that heterosexuality is the preferred sexual preference within modern Witchcraft. I understand those concerns, but my gods have always been gay, straight, and everything in between.

I prefer to see the symbolic Great Rite as a celebration of union or joining. Anytime two lovers get together, they create something new, and besides, most of us don't engage in sexual relations just to make a baby. For me, the Great Rite is about two forces coming together. It's easy to see those forces as male and female, but I look at them in other ways too. They could be land and sky, water and earth, stardust and solar wind. We live in a pretty magical universe, and worlds, life, and stars are all created in a variety of different ways. When performing the Great Rite, I tend to think about all of those things in circle.

In our coven we use a rather simple version of the Great Rite, focused on the "magick of joining" and how two different forces can combine to create a new one. The symbolic Great Rite is more than just dunking a knife into a cup of wine, juice, or water; it's a celebration of the forces that create life, pleasure, and everything we cherish in this existence. While holding the athame or chalice, it's important to visualize all of those things. That's where the magick and mystery truly happen.

I write ritual with my wife and me in mind (which is why everything is usually labeled "high priestess" and "high priest"), but such titles aren't necessary, and I have happily performed the Great Rite with a coven brother on many occasions. During ritual I try to make my movements and gestures as "big" as possible. Drama isn't necessary in ritual, but I believe it can make ritual better, so lift that athame up high when performing the Great Rite! Our version of the Great Rite often plays out in this way:

High Priest: *We are surrounded by life and breath, reminding us of the greatest of magics—the magick of joining!*

High Priestess: *Sun and rain, soil and breeze, all must unite to create the living upon this earth!*

High Priest: *The athame is a part of creation.*

High Priestess: *As the chalice is a part of creation.*

Both: *United, they bring forth new life. Blessed be!*
(Athame is plunged into chalice.)

In some traditions, the individual holding the chalice then licks the athame. My wife has always worried about cutting her tongue on my blade, so we've always skipped that step. It does look impressive though.

Immediately after the Great Rite, my coven celebrates the feast of cakes and ale (or cakes and wine). We haven't used ale during a ritual in many years, but we've stuck with the phrase. Cakes and ale is an old English phrase meaning "the good things in life." Whatever food and drink you choose to use for cakes and ale is immaterial. What's important is that everyone in your ritual finds them to be "good." The Goddess and the God want us to be happy, and what we eat and drink in ritual should express that idea.

Cakes and ale is a mini-feast, and I use my athame to bless both food and drink. Many covens use the wine blessed during the Great Rite for their "ale." During ritual, my coven generally uses two chalices. The one we use for the ceremonial Great Rite is saved for libations after ritual. We then take up a separate chalice, fill it with drink, then bless it with the athame, touching the side of the glass or perhaps the chalice's rim. We do things this way because our athames sometimes get a little dirty with the mixing of salt and water, etc. Whatever way you choose will work just fine. While touching the cup with the athame, imagine energy leaving the athame and entering the drink, canceling out any negativity and putting some of that "energy of creation" into the beverage.

I do basically the same thing with whatever "cakes" we are consuming that night, touching each one with the point of my athame and visualizing them being charged and cleansed. While touching the cakes and drink, we usually recite a blessing over them:

Lord and Lady, bless this food and drink set out before us. May each bite and sip remind us of your love, beauty, and abundance. So mote it be!

We then pass the food and drink around the circle, making sure to save some for libations later. (My wife would like me to point out that, for the sake of cleanliness, the drink should be passed out before the food, especially when using a shared communal cup. No one wants a crumb of bread floating in their wine.)

A Door to the Summerlands

In many Witchcraft traditions, it's customary to call upon the "Mighty Dead" in ritual. The Mighty Dead are our Witch ancestors, known and unknown, who watch over us and sometimes assist us in our rites. Some groups simply call the Mighty Dead to them, while others open up a portal to the Summerlands[16] in order to bring the dead into the circle. The athame is the essential tool for those looking to create an entryway into the realm of spirit.

Doors to the Summerlands are generally constructed in the west, home to the "spirits of death and initiation," but are also sometimes created in the north. If I'm creating an entryway into the Summerlands, I tend to do so after casting the

16 I think of the Summerlands as a sort of cosmic waiting room where souls go between incarnations on this earth. It's not quite "heaven," but it's similar.

circle and calling the quarters but before inviting the gods to be a part of my rite.

To create a portal to the Summerlands, stand in the west and envision the energies of the circle moving around you. At about shoulder level, slash at the circle and focus on the Summerlands. Interpretations on what the land of the dead looks like vary wildly, but I see my window into it as dark and gray, like a giant storm cloud. Hold that thought in your mind and begin carving out a small window-shaped space in the circle. While carving that space out, say the following words:

I seek the spirits of the Mighty Dead. Beloved ancestors, join us here in our rites. Bless us with your love, knowledge, and power. All who would seek to aid me in my rites are welcome here. Those who wish me or my fellows harm are not allowed in this space!

When calling to the Mighty Dead, it's acceptable to say the name of a loved one or a teacher/mentor in the Craft. That doesn't ensure that they will show up; it should be an invitation and not a demand. Once the portal to the Summerlands is open, pay special attention to the energies coming out of it. If something negative feels like it's trying to get through, push against it with the athame, forcing it back into the Summerlands. Calling to the spirits of the dead can be dangerous work. There are negative spirits out there who might seek to hinder your work, so be ready for them.

After the portal has been created, the magician has three options. The portal can be kept open for the duration of the ritual, which is a dangerous plan since more spirits and energies might come through it. It can be closed but left open, like a window with the curtains pulled back. This serves as a reminder that just outside the realm of the living always lies the realm of the dead. This option has consequences, as it might attract a negative spirit; even the souls of the dead aren't averse to peeking through an open window. The best option is to close the portal using the athame.

To close the portal, first picture the window into the Summerlands closing and then push that energy away using the athame as the focus of the push. Next, imagine the thundercloud of the next realm breaking up and dissipating. Sometimes at the end of this I see a ray of sunshine pour down from the sky. Finally, focus again on the magick circle; see the threads and weaves of energy used in its creation and imagine knitting them back together. I often use my athame to pick up the individual threads and weave them back together. When I have closed the portal, I say:

The Athame in Ritual

The portal is now closed. All who have arrived in this space have done so in good faith. We welcome the Mighty Dead to our rite. Hail and welcome!

I usually kiss my blade here as a sign of welcoming.

If the Mighty Dead have arrived at your ritual through a door to the Summerlands, it's very important to open that door and allow them to return to their plane of existence. Creating the portal for the return journey is the same as creating it at the start, but with different words. This time you'll want to say goodbye and make sure everybody finds the door. Feel the energy of the Mighty Dead around you and make sure to push them toward the door if they don't actively seek it. As before, make sure nothing unwanted comes through when the portal is open again. Dismiss them, saying these words:

Beloved ancestors, Mighty Dead, we thank you for joining us in our rites! Now we bid you farewell and offer you safe return to the Summerlands. Until we meet again we will keep you in our hearts and minds. Hail and farewell!

After a hearty "hail and farewell," I blow them another kiss. I bid farewell to the Mighty Dead after thanking the Goddess and the God for being a part of our rite and before dismissing the quarters, though you can bid the Mighty Dead farewell at any point in ritual. What's most important is that the goodbye is heartfelt and makes sense to you in the flow of the ritual. Make sure the doorway to the lands of the dead is properly sealed and all is "as it once was" before moving on and finishing up the ritual.

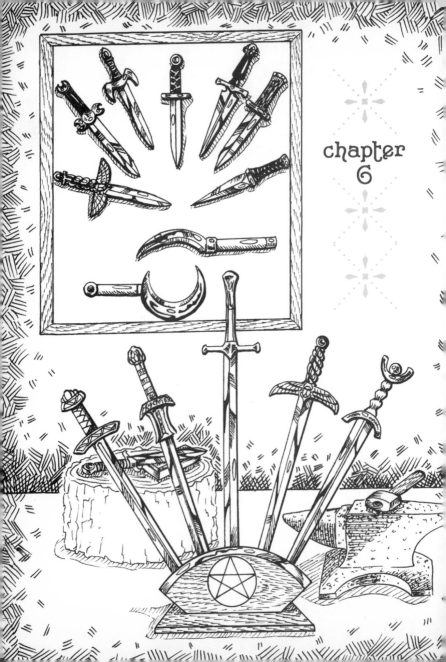

chapter
6

The Boline and the White-Handled Knife

The first modern Witches generally used three different knives in their practices. The first was, of course, the athame, and it was seldom if ever used for any actual physical cutting. For physical cutting, most Witches used the unimaginatively titled *white-handled knife*, sometimes called a *kerfan* (or *kirfane*). A third sickle-shaped or slightly curved knife called a *boline*, generally used for cutting herbs and other plants, rounded out the trio.

As the years have gone by, the white-handled knife and the boline have essentially merged into one tool, with many Witches unaware that their altars once contained a *kerfan* knife. The standard athame has also absorbed many of the functions once carried out by the white-handled knife. There are still many Witches and traditions of Witchcraft that continue to use all three knives, but that's become more and more rare.

Originally the Witch's toolbox contained two ritual knives. There was the athame (to be used when calling the quarters, casting the circle, and celebrating the Great Rite) and the kirfane (used for everything else). White-handled knives were used for marking candles, creating other tools, cutting cords, and any other physical activity that might take place inside the circle. In time, many Witches began to feel completely comfortable using their athames for what were essentially magical acts, and discontinued their use of the kirfane.

The boline (sometimes spelled *bolline* and generally pronounced "bow-leen" or "bow-line") bears some similarities to the white-handled knife, but it was originally designed for entirely different work. Like the white-handled knife, the traditional boline has a white handle, but that's where the similarities end. The boline is sickle-shaped, resembling the traditional Druid's tool more than a Witch's knife. The boline was also designed to be used outside (or perhaps in an indoor garden) and not in the Witch's circle. The kirfane was originally a ritual tool that sat on the altar as a complement to the athame.

At some point, the white-handled knife was superseded by the boline, though no one is exactly sure why. Perhaps the idea of three knives simply seemed redundant. Any cutting that was needed could be done with the boline (or even the athame) and besides, the boline was completely unique. It has that cool shape and stands in sharp contrast to the athame.

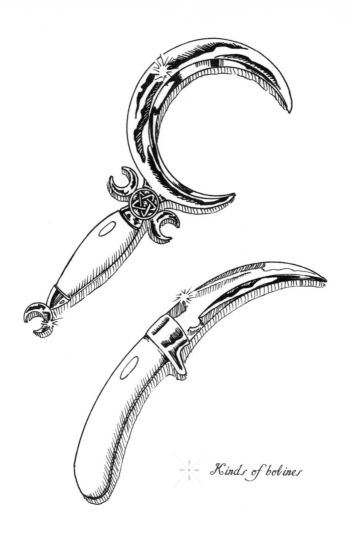

Kinds of bolines

The Boline and the White-Handled Knife

In many traditions the kirfane wasn't a reverse-athame; it had its own specifications besides the white handle. Instead of a double-sided blade, it often had just one cutting edge. Its point was also kept as sharp as possible, all the more effective for carving into candles or other magical aids. There are some spells and rituals in this book that call for actual physical cutting; for the purists out there who would never sully their athames in such a way, they can all be done with the white-handled knife.

If you own more than one athame, it's possible that you are already using one of your knives as a kirfane. I use one of my athames for most of my ritual "cutting" needs and another one for all the symbolic stuff. Until I wrote this book, it never would have occurred to me that one of those blades is closer to the "white-handled knife" than the traditional athame.

Both the boline and the kirfane are rather modern innovations, though they have a long history. Not surprisingly, a word very close to *boline* shows up in the *Key of Solomon*, which contains a whole host of knives. Among them, there is the *bolino*, a needle-like knife that doesn't look like a boline or a kirfane. In chapter 2 of his *Book of Ceremonial Magic* (1915), Christian occultist A. E. Waite refers to a *"bolline* or sickle" and includes a drawing of the tool, which looks like a small fish-hook-shaped knife.

Waite refers to his bolline as the "most important" of a magician's tools and includes instructions for making a bolline:

> The most important to make is that called the bolline; it must be forged on the day and in the hour of Jupiter, selecting a small piece of unused steel. Set it thrice in the fire and extinguish it in the blood of a mole mixed with the juice of the pimpernel. Let this be done when the Moon is in her full light and course. On the same day and in the hour of Jupiter, fit a horn handle to the steel, shaping it with a new sword forged thrice as above in the fire.

I have little doubt that the origin of the boline in modern Witchcraft comes from Waite. Today's boline doesn't much resemble Waite's drawing of the "boline or sickle," but it certainly matches how most of us envision a sickle.

Most bolines today have stainless steel blades, though brass is a popular alternative (and visually striking). A friend of mine suggested a boline with a ceramic blade. Ceramic is great for cutting soft vegetables since it can be made extremely sharp. The downside is that a ceramic blade is not very strong; you certainly wouldn't want to use it to saw through anything.

Another bonus is that a ceramic boline could have both a white blade and a white handle. Since it's a knife, it's generally associated with the element of fire (or sometimes air), but since I use mine almost exclusively outdoors, I think of it more as a tool of earth.

Many Witch traditions have specifications for the boline that are similar to those for the athame. They call for a white wooden handle, but this is a qualification I see less and less often today. Besides, practicality matters more than tradition. A boline handle can be any color and made from any material you are comfortable with. I do think that because the blade is designed specifically for cutting, it should always be made of metal (instead of wood, stone, or bone), but I'm sure there are some who object to that.

I've always been hesitant to use my boline in ritual because its purpose is so very different from that of the athame (or even the traditional white-handled knife). To put it simply, the boline is a tool of death. It's used to harvest plants, and is often the instrument that ends their lives. Because of that, I prefer to keep it out of my rituals and often my spellwork. It doesn't make any sense to me to use a tool that causes death in a healing ritual, for example. I think the early Witches made a very wise decision by separating the athame from the boline.

While researching this book, I found plenty of instances where bolines and white-handled knives were used interchangeably during ritual. I'm not sure many of those Witches stopped to reflect on the symbolism and different energies those knives were originally intended to have. If you are comfortable with using your boline in circle, by all means feel free to use it, but I'm a bit wary of the idea.

Finding a Boline

I think there's a pretty good amount of wiggle room when it comes to finding the right boline. Though I've always preferred a sickle-shaped blade, many Witches own a boline that has only a slight curve to the blade. Because there's no set rule on the blade, the boline can go beyond mere knife.

I know some Witches whose bolines are simply basic knives whose use is reserved for things outside the circle. The blades aren't curved and the handles aren't white; they are simply effective cutting tools, though tools that are charged and consecrated. Since the boline is more personal than other tools, this makes a lot of sense. Since we don't bring our bolines to ritual, there's no one around to tell people that their boline is "wrong."

Knives with a curved blade are easy enough to find at knife stores and even at some metaphysical/Witch shops. To be honest, single-sided blades are often easier to find than double-sided ones. What's probably most important when it comes to choosing a boline is how sharp it is. Since it's going to be used for actual cutting, it's important to have a knife that's more practical than ornamental. I've handled many athames over the years that weren't sharp enough to cut through a stick of butter, but that won't work with the boline. It has to be sharp.

Because I use my boline extensively in the garden, mine isn't even a proper knife. It's actually more akin to a hand sickle. This means I can't use it in the kitchen for chopping or slicing anything, but it works amazingly well outside. I love the idea of using something that ancient Druids might have used, and I like that it makes my boline completely unique from my other knives.

If you plan to use your boline a lot in the garden, hand sickles can be purchased at most hardware stores. Effective ones can be picked up for as little as ten dollars, but since it's going to be both a garden and a magical tool, I suggest spending a little extra money and getting a really good one. When it comes to the boline, what's really important is finding one that works for you.

Blessing a Boline

As a Witch's tool, the boline is unique. It's the only "standard" Witch tool that's not designed to be used in ritual space. Bolines are meant to be used outdoors in nature (or at least our gardens). Since the boline as a tool exists "between the worlds," I think it requires an extra blessing in addition to the usual consecration.

Before blessing your boline, consecrate it as you would an athame (there's a ritual for that in chapter 4). Once it's been consecrated, the only extra tool you'll need for this boline blessing is a bowl of water. Start by taking the water and your curved knife to wherever you think your boline will get the most use. For those of us lucky enough to have a garden, this is probably where you'd want to perform this ritual. If you have a container garden, your potted plants are an ideal spot too.

Place the blade of the boline into the ground. Get as deep into the earth as you possibly can; if you can bury your boline up to the hilt, all the better. Place your hand on the boline's handle and feel the energy of the earth coming up through it. Let your consciousness drift for a second and let your energy mingle with that of the earth, moving down through the handle, into the blade, and into the ground. As you drift downward, feel the embrace of the Goddess in the earth and the touch of the God coming from the sun.

The Boline and the White-Handled Knife

Acknowledge them both while saying:

From the power of the sky and the energy of the earth comes new life. When those great powers unite, the magick of creation begins. I thank the Lord and the Lady for their blessings.

Look up at the sky and then back down at your boline. Think about how you will be using this tool in the months and years to come. Envision yourself harvesting herbs, vegetables, and fruit. See it as a sacred tool of the harvest and as a link to all of the Pagans and Witches who have come before you. Imagine yourself using it in a responsible manner and say:

I pledge to harvest only what I need, no more, no less. I will not waste, so therefore I will not want. May my boline be a tool of balance that keeps me in harmony with nature.

Now take your bowl or chalice of water and slowly pour the water into the earth around your boline while saying:

What I take, I shall return. I am a part of the web, not the master of it. With this boline I will reap what I have sown, and I shall do so with appreciation and humility. May the earth drink deeply from this cup I share!

Pull the boline up from the earth and set it on the ground. Take some dirt and sprinkle it on the blade and ask the Goddess for her blessings:

Great Mother, Earth Goddess, bless this blade so that it might bring me closer to your mysteries. So mote it be!

Now hold up the blade so it reflects the rays of the sun and ask the God to also bless your boline:

Horned One, Lord of the Forest, bless this blade so that it might bring me closer to your creation. So mote it be!

After receiving the blessings of the Lord and the Lady, your boline should now be ready for use.

Using a Boline

The ideal place for using a boline is outdoors. I use mine to harvest fruit, vegetables, herbs, and anything else growing that needs to be cut or pruned. Since using a boline in such a manner requires "taking" from nature, it's usually a good idea to thank whatever you are harvesting.

When harvesting from a tree, I tend to talk directly to the tree and thank it for the fruit that it has produced. In addition

The Boline and the White-Handled Knife

to thanking the tree, I also like to present it with a little gift. I know many Witches who leave coins or other such goodies, but I've always preferred to be practical. I like to give my trees some fertilizer or a good, overly indulgent drink of water. I think they appreciate that more.

Sometimes harvesting something means ending the life of a particular plant. I admit, I sometimes feel guilty when I have to basically kill a plant. In such cases I tend to approach the plant reverently and with a deep sense of thanks. I also promise that I will honor the gifts they've given and will welcome back their descendants next spring. Many of the plants I harvest are annuals, meaning they typically die over the course of one growing season, so I think they are prepared for what's coming. Still, I do shed a tear each year when I pluck the last pumpkin from the vine.

Before harvest time I often use my boline when digging around in my garden/yard and pruning the plants and flowers within it. Since my boline is a consecrated and charged magical tool, I think it adds a little bit of energy to my gardening experience. It also makes harvesting plants and working outdoors a sacred and holy experience.

Being a Witch means being outdoors and within nature. For many of us, getting to truly "wild" land isn't possible, but growing some tomatoes in a pot or keeping a small herb garden in the kitchen is. Using my boline for such projects reminds me that growing things is a valid and often necessary witchy endeavor. My boline connects me to nature in ways that my other tools do not.

If your boline is more a traditional knife than a moon-shaped blade, there's no harm in using it in the kitchen. There's something magical about the idea of using a tool from planting to harvest to slow cooker. There are several spells in this book that call for the athame in the kitchen, but in a lot of ways the boline is an even better choice.

Ancient Druids and the Sickle

The second largest modern Pagan tradition is most likely Druidry, and it's popular on both sides of the Atlantic Ocean and many other spots throughout the world. Druidry bears a close resemblance to modern Witchcraft because there's been a lot of sharing between the two traditions. Many of the most famous Druids of the past fifty years have also practiced the Craft. There's been a lot of give and take between the two groups over the last hundred years, and that's likely to continue into the future.

Modern Druidry exists in two forms. There are Druids who actively attempt to recreate the rituals of the ancient Celts in a modern context, along with Druid groups whose roots can be traced back to the types of fellowship first pioneered by the Freemasons and other fraternal orders. Neither type claims to be a direct continuation of ancient Druidry, though both

The Boline and the White-Handled Knife

kinds of Druids certainly respect and admire their long-ago forbearers.

We don't know exactly what the Druids of two thousand years ago practiced, but some of their rites have been passed down to us by writers of the period. One of the most famous passages concerning Druids was written by the naturalist and historian Pliny the Elder (23–79 CE). Pliny's description of Druids in white robes gathering mistletoe under the full moon has been an inspiration to many artists and modern Druids, and is one of the most compelling pictures of ancient Druid practice.

Pliny's mention of Druids appears in his massive book *Natural History* in a section about mistletoe. His description of Druids is so captivating that it's the most famous part of his work. In book 16, chapter 95, of *Natural History*, he writes:

> Upon this occasion we must not omit to mention the admiration that is lavished upon this plant by the Gauls. The Druids—for that is the name they give to their magicians—held nothing more sacred than the mistletoe and the tree that bears it... The mistletoe, however, is but rarely found upon the robur [oak tree]; and when found, is gathered with rites replete with religious awe... This day they select because the moon,

though not yet in the middle of her course, has already considerable power and influence; and they call her by a name which signifies, in their language, the all-healing. Having made all due preparation for the sacrifice and a banquet beneath the trees, they bring thither two white bulls, the horns of which are bound then for the first time. Clad in a white robe the priest ascends the tree, and cuts the mistletoe with a golden sickle, which is received by others in a white cloak. They then immolate the victims, offering up their prayers that God will render this gift of his propitious to those to whom he has so granted it.

Of most interest to us is the use of the golden sickle in the mistletoe-gathering rite.

Pliny's Druids are obviously using a ceremonial sickle. If the blade they used was truly "golden," it seems unlikely that it was being used on a daily basis. The modern boline is similar to the sickle, and many bolines today also have the curved blade generally associated with the sickle.

As tantalizing as Pliny's tale is, there are no other Greek or Roman writers who mention a ceremonial Druid sickle. It's also possible that Pliny's information on Druids isn't quite accurate. Pliny is a rather reliable historian when writing about

The Boline and the White-Handled Knife

things close to his home in Rome, but a bit less so the further afield his subjects are. For instance, he populated the Sahara Desert with a people he called the Blemmyis, who were headless and had their eyes and mouths on their chests.[17]

Even with Pliny's limitations, as a travel writer the passage quoted here likely offers some real insights into the Druids. The Celts did honor mistletoe and oak trees and practice animal sacrifice. The "golden sickle" is a bit more suspect, but I suspect a sickle was present, though I'm not sure how golden it would have been (especially if it was used during sacrifices).

Today's Druids don't sacrifice animals and I've never seen one climb an oak tree in a white robe, but a few of them still use sickles in their rituals. Druid groups operate differently from most witchy ones, and most Druids today are members of large international organizations. Druids might be smaller in number than today's Witches, but they are often better organized.

North America's largest Druid organization, Ár nDraíocht Féin (A Druid Fellowship, generally known as ADF), doesn't use the sickle at all. The Henge of Keltria, an offshoot of ADF, does still use the sickle, but only occasionally. The biggest Druid group in the world, the Order of Bards, Ovates, and

---

17 Ronald Hutton, *Blood and Mistletoe: The History of the Druids in Britain* (New Haven, CT: Yale University Press, 2009), p. 15. For a history of the Druids from antiquity to the modern age, there is no better resource than this great book.

Druids (OBOD), has much in common with modern Witch-craft. OBOD Druids call quarters and cast circles, but they do so without a sword, an athame, or even a sickle. So while Druids have a long history with pointy things, the modern variety doesn't use them all that much.

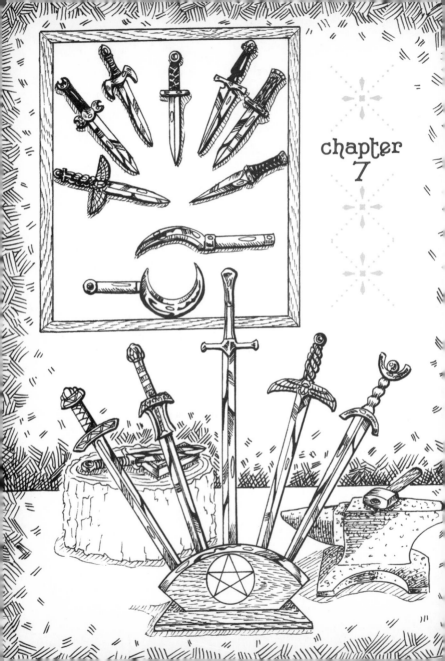

chapter
7

The Athame in the Kitchen

To use the athame outside of circle or not to use the athame out of the circle... it's not *the* question, but it's a common one. When I began my journey into Witchcraft, I was a firm believer that using my athame as much as possible would make it a more effective tool. During that period of time, I used it for all sorts of activities: cooking, sewing, and even a little bit of cleaning. Today, I still use one of my athames for some of these tasks, and I'm not alone.

For every Witch who disagrees with the idea of using the athame for common physical tasks, there's another Witch actively using the athame in just such a fashion. Since I own a few blades, I've split the difference in recent years, but I completely understand the reasoning for wanting to use an athame as much as possible. Every time we touch and use our athames, they become more in tune with us. Using an athame in the kitchen is a proactive approach and can also be fun.

It's empowering to turn dinnertime into a ritual. Eating is an act we perform on a number of levels. We have to eat to survive, but we also eat for pure pleasure. Eating has also been a religious act since the start of religion. Whipping the old athame out on a Sunday evening turns an ordinary act into a sacred one. My athame radiates energy, so why not transfer some of that energy into my dinner? This can be an especially good pick-me-up on a rotten day.

An alternative to using a ritual athame in the kitchen is simply to bless and consecrate one's kitchen knives. In many ways my kitchen knives are like a second set of athames. My bread knife has been a part of my life for ten years now, slicing up thick loaves of bread at holiday feasts and on lazy Saturday mornings. I'm attached to my kitchen knives much as I'm attached to my athames, and I can't imagine ever buying a new paring knife or even a new set of steak knives. Cooking is much like an act of magick: it's a transformative experience, so it shouldn't be a surprise that kitchen implements often feel like magical tools when in our hands.

I don't have any athame-specific recipes to share in this book. I simply use my athame in the kitchen when I think the situation calls for it. When I'm baking for the coven or making a dish for a ritual feast, I'm far more likely to make it a part of my kitchen tasks. I'm also more apt to use my athame in the kitchen if I'm cooking a special meal for family or friends (like at Thanksgiving). I've never used my athame to finely cut meat, but it's a serviceable tool for chopping vegetables and making decorative marks on top of certain items. The sky is the limit when it comes to the athame in the kitchen, with the only real limit being your imagination and the sharpness of your blade.

Infusing Food with Energy

When I want to use my athame in the kitchen and just can't think of a practical way to do so, I simply use it to project energy into food. If you are someone who doesn't like to use your athame in "Kitchen Witch" situations, this technique doesn't require you to touch your athame to anything either. It can also be used for anything you are cooking.

The best time to add energy to a dish is before baking. Cooking generally melds flavors together, so adding energy to a meal before cooking it allows that energy to permeate the entire entrée. If I'm going for a big infusion of energy, I like to add a little ritual drama to the proceedings to focus my intent and remind myself of the seriousness of the endeavor.

I start by raising my athame over my head and saying:

My will and desire go into this dish.
Cooking fire and ancient art, release this wish.
Infuse this meal with power and might.
Empower my will and my tongue delight.
With athame I cast my Wiccan power,
This meal my coven will devour!

If I'm using an athame that I utilize only for (non-physical) ritual work, I simply hold it over whatever I'm preparing and direct my energy into it. Oftentimes, though, I'll simply dip my athame directly into what I'm cooking. I probably look a bit ridiculous with my left arm raised over my head and my right hand plunging my athame into a bowl of cake batter, but I like the results. Putting a dash of magick into food is a great way to share a little energy and ensure that it goes directly into the body.

Breads and Pastries

The ceremony of cakes and ale is an important part of ritual, and is even more powerful when using homemade baked goods. At Ostara (the spring equinox), I serve hot cross buns to my coven every year, and I always mark those buns with a solar cross. It's pretty simple to do and gives me a good excuse to use my athame in the kitchen. Before baking the buns, I simply slash a Celtic-style cross into the soft dough. While making my slash, I say a quick spell over every cake:

> *Equal day and equal night,*
> *Strive ever toward the light!*

Crosses are easy to make, especially when I have limited space to work in. When baking a loaf of bread, I usually attempt to make a pentagram on top of the loaf. This works best when making a round loaf of bread, but a pentagram can even be carved into an oblong sort of shape. When crafting a pentagram onto a loaf of bread, I try to use the symbol of the invoking pentagram, which brings energies closer to us. When I eat a piece of bread, I'm trying to bring nutrients and sustenance into my body, so I think the use of the invoking pentagram makes a great deal of sense.

It takes five slashes of the athame to make a pentagram, and since I bake only one loaf of bread for the coven, I find there's time to linger over every line I carve into the bread.

Since five distinct lines match up nicely with the four elements (earth, air, fire, water) and the binding force of spirit, I invoke those forces while carving my pentagram:

> *From the east to inspire,*
> *From the south and desire,*
> *From the west with emotion,*

From the north and devotion,
Bound by spirit the elements dwell
In my bread by Witch's spell.
So mote it be!

When my pentagram-clad bread comes out of the oven looking extra impressive, I make sure everyone in the coven gets a good look at it. There's nothing wrong with taking a bit of pride in your work.

Soups and Stews

There's something very witchy about a large pot of boiling soup or stew. The biggest pot in my kitchen doesn't look all that much like a cauldron, but during the winter when I leave it on the stove to simmer for a few hours, it gets pretty close. Cutting up vegetables and setting them to boil just *feels* like something a medieval Witch might have done, so when I get a chance to do this, I step right into the role.

Nothing makes me feel more witchy than a chanted spell, and when cooking up a stew, this is the one I use:

Double, double toil and trouble,
Fire burn and cauldron bubble.
Finger of orange, apple of earth,
Set to boil upon the hearth.

A dash of salt, a pinch of pepper,
Go gently with the Allium cepa.
Infused with magick and might,
Make this my dinner tonight.

In case you were wondering, *finger of orange* refers to carrots, and *apple of earth* is the literal translation of the French *pomme de terre,* apple of the earth, which refers to potatoes. *Allium cepa* is the Latin phrase for onion, and since I'm not a fan of onions, I go easy on them while cooking. The beginning comes from Shakespeare's *Macbeth* and usually results in a chuckle from my wife if she overhears me incanting a spell over dinner!

Cleansing Your Home

Outside of ritual I often use my athame to spiritually cleanse my house. The next time you do a little bit of spring cleaning, remember to do a little psychic cleaning as well to remove any bad energy from your home or workspace. Cleansing your personal space is especially recommended if you are moving into a new house or apartment. There's a bumper sticker that says, "Take a Whammy from my Athame," and it's a phrase I hold to when using my knife to cleanse my home.

I start all of my home cleanings at the front door since that's where most energy enters the house. I like to end the cleansing at my back door, but if you don't have a back door, I suggest a kitchen window or a patio door. The main objective of a home cleansing using the athame is to stir up any negative energies in your home and push them away. I usually scoot them all out a window or door, but if the energy is especially dark, you might have to break it up into smaller pieces before sweeping it away.

Before you start, you'll want to focus on the task at hand and visualize it in your mind's eye. See yourself moving through your house projecting a cleansing blue flame from your athame. Feel the fire from your blade full of powerful energy and charging everything around you with positivity. Because I want my home to match my own energies, I use the power of my magical will for this particular operation.

Start at your front door and begin projecting energy from your athame with a sweeping motion. In a lot of ways you are "psychically sweeping," so you'll want to move the energy coming from your athame much like you would move a broom. Visualize everything the blue energy from your blade touches becoming clean and pristine. I'm usually unable to "see" negative energy, but I can almost always feel it. When I'm projecting magick for cleansing, I visualize that negative energy I'm sweeping up as a sort of cosmic dust. I can see it bouncing along the ground as I sweep it toward an open window and away from me.

Unlike dust, negative energy can be anywhere in a home, so it's important to go over every inch of space, including the walls and the ceiling. I always pay a little extra attention to the corners of every room because that's often where forgotten things and energies congregate. Sometimes I see the power coming from my athame "blasting out" the psychic dirt that accumulates in my house. After a good thump of energy, I sweep up the scattered pieces of energy and get rid of them.

Words aren't necessary when cleansing your house, but they sometimes serve as a good focal point for magick and can assist in maintaining focus. Every time I enter a new room during my spring cleaning, I loudly say:

Only good shall reside in this space.
I cleanse and consecrate this place.
By my power I make this room right,
Full of my energy, passion, and light!

When I sweep the last few bits of negative detritus out the window, I usually say a few more words:

All that's dark and gray, I now cast far away!
Cleansed by the athame's fire,
Fueled by my heart's desire!
This space shall serve me, so mote it be!

If the area you are cleaning has been hit by tragedy, you may have to take more drastic measures to rid it of negative energy. My wife and I once bought a house that someone had been stabbed in. The room where the stabbing occurred (in the creepy basement, of course) was full of really negative energy, and it took us a while to get rid of it. When you come across energy like that, it is very hard to get rid of.

Unlike most bits of negative energy, the big pieces are more like giant boulders than dust that can be swept up. When you come across those big chunks of energy, you'll want to break them up. I do that by focusing on the area of negativity and then sending out a projected and concentrated beam of energy from my athame. Visualize the energy from your knife shooting into the accumulated bad energy. Keep "blasting" it until it breaks into several smaller pieces. Once you've broken up the accumulated dark energy, it should be easy to sweep outside.

Sometimes getting rid of the energy left over from a traumatic experience can take a few attempts. If that happens, you aren't a failure as a Witch; it's just that some operations take longer than others. Keep attacking the accumulated mass of negative energy every few days. Think of it as chipping away at a rock—no one chips away an entire boulder in a day.

Death and violence aren't the only sources of negative energy. Our own energies sometimes play a role too. If you are under a great deal of stress or have a lot of anger in your heart, it will accumulate. Before attempting to psychically sweep your house, try to fix those issues first. It will be hard to make any progress with your home if you haven't made any progress with yourself.

Keep repeating all the cleansing steps as you move through your home. In difficult areas (like a basement), you may have to move the energy up a set of stairs before you can deposit it outside. Speaking of outside, don't forget to cleanse your yard and porch too! If you don't have a lot of privacy, you may want to wait until late evening to cleanse your outdoor spaces so your neighbors don't see you waving around your athame in the front yard. On the other hand, letting your neighbors see you swing around your athame might be a good deterrent!

GETTING TO THE POINT
Jenya T. Beachy

THERE IS ONE particular use of the magickal knife that's rarely talked about. For many Witches, kitchen-style and otherwise,

The Athame in the Kitchen

the most important tool is the one that has the most power. In my house, that tool is the Alpha Hunter produced by the Buck Company. That's the knife we use when we harvest our own meat.

We are not hunters; we don't go out to test our skills against the wilderness. We raise the animals we slaughter, from rabbits to chickens, and fill our freezer with creatures that have grown up in our care.

The gods we honor don't demand this sacrifice. It's for our human bellies that we unsheathe that ritual blade. It's toward a greater responsibility for those things who fall for our rising. We have, all of us, an opportunity to become closer to the practices and processes that go into our lifestyle.

The athame has become known for its use as a cutter of energetic space. Knives were originally made for one purpose: to separate this from that. In our family practice, we are separating a spirit from physical reality. We free the molecules of this creature to become part of us, to move back into the rhythm of the universe from which it was originally made.

Later, we will fall to the blade of Death and go to feed the world that we loved so well.

Blessed be our sacrifice.

Jenya T. Beachy
www.jenyatbeachy.com

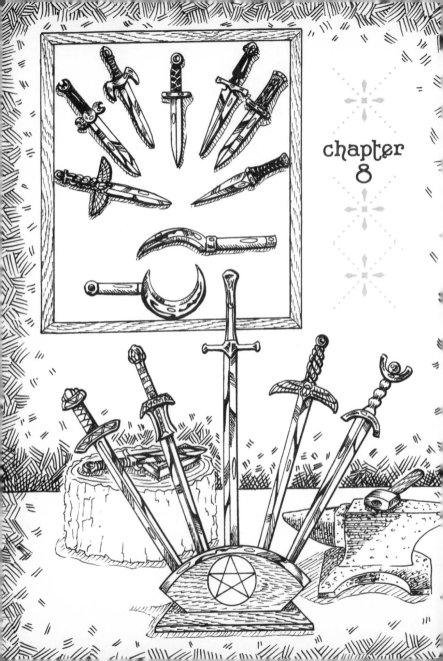

chapter 8

The Sword

The first draft of this book included only a 500-word subsection on the sword. When my editor offered her initial critiques of this book, one of them was, "Why didn't you write more about the sword?" Good question. *Why wasn't I writing more about the sword?* I love my ritual sword just as much as I love my athames, and it's been a part of my rituals on both sides of the United States. (I've always wondered what TSA, the Transportation Safety Administration, thinks when they find my sword in my checked luggage.) So what *was* my initial reasoning for not including a lengthy bit on the sword?

The athame and the sword are inexorably linked. Everything one can do with an athame one can do with a sword, and vice versa. Would enacting the Great Rite with a sword be a bit difficult? Sure, but it would also be completely acceptable. In many ways, a Witch's ritual sword is simply an extremely long athame, but there's also a bit about it that's fundamentally different.

Almost every Witch I know owns an athame. A smaller but still sizable number own a boline. Those two blades are common and easily obtainable, especially the athame. Most Witches I know don't own a sword. Due to their size, swords are fundamentally more expensive, and more difficult to simply hide away. It's hard to find a fitting space for a ritual sword in a one-room apartment or a dorm room. Can it be done? Certainly, but it's a lot harder.

Even some of my teachers and mentors, people who have been practicing the Craft for three decades or more, don't own a sword. I've been a part of covens where everyone brings their athame to ritual, but that's never happened with a sword. It's expected that I own an athame, but my swords are seen as a bonus.

So the scarcity of the sword is one of the reasons I initially chose not to write very much about it, but that's not the only reason. Swords are also often shared by a coven, and used sparingly. In my own coven, we use the sword specifically for casting the circle, and nothing else. The sword we use has been in my possession for eighteen years, but it feels less like my sword at this point and more like it belongs to the coven. In a legal sense I "own" the sword we use in ritual, but I'm rarely the one who wields it in coven situations. There are

Witch covens that have been operating for over fifty years, and their sword is continually passed down from high priestess to high priestess. Imagine a sword with fifty years of history, not with one individual but with one group, being wielded by perhaps dozens of Witches over the decades!

This is in sharp contrast to the athame, a tool so personal that most Witches ask before picking up another Witch's blade. People sometimes ask to borrow my sword depending on the situation, but no one has ever asked to borrow one of my athames. This is the primary reason I was initially reluctant to write about swords in this book. There's a big difference between the two tools: one is primarily a personal working tool and the other is often shared and used by a variety of individuals.

I often think of the sword as a tool of "high magick," meaning that it's more likely to turn up in a circle practicing ceremonial magick than in a coven of Witches. The tools of the Witch are generally easily obtainable (and easily hidden) objects. For much of their history, swords were generally only in the possession of soldiers or individuals with a lot of money.

There's also a level of seriousness that seems to accompany the sword. In the Golden Dawn, the sword "is to be used in all cases where great force and strength are required, but principally for banishing and for defense against evil forces." [18]

---

18   Israel Regardie, *The Golden Dawn*, 6th ed. (St. Paul, MN: Llewellyn Publications, 1989), p. 317.

The Sword

I've always taken my athame seriously, but I've never thought of it quite in those terms.

When I use my sword in ritual, it tends to attract a lot of attention, more so than my knife. Part of this might be because it's old in a way that the rest of my tools are not. I have trouble imagining using an eighty-year-old chalice in ritual, but it just feels right that my sword is over a hundred years old. Crafted in Toledo, Spain, back in 1910, my sword is the only ritual tool I own whose history is a complete mystery to me. Was it used during the Spanish Civil War or in the rituals of a Masonic lodge? Just how did it end up in Detroit, Michigan, with my friend Dwayne, who gave it to me? There's no other tool I use on a regular basis where such questions would be acceptable, but it feels right with my sword.

Due to its age and (presumed) large number of unknown caretakers, my sword has a certain weariness not shared by my other tools. Everything else I own is in remarkably good condition, but my sword is beaten up and probably a bit rusty. There are several knocks on the blade where it looks like someone tried to use it to chop down a tree. It's not sharp enough to cut through warm butter, but it always feels right in my hands. For all of its issues, it also has some beautiful scrollwork etched into the blade and has a solidity to it not often found in this day and age.

My old and slightly battered sword

The Sword

My sword looks like it's been on a journey and has a story to tell, and in that sense it's very much like a lot of swords throughout history. Few weapons have inspired such love and devotion as the sword. Everyone is familiar with King Arthur and his sword Excalibur. Nearly as well known is Sting, the sword of hobbit Bilbo Baggins, and fans of modern fantasy probably recall that Arya Stark's sword is named Needle. (Arya is a character in *Game of Thrones* and steals every scene she's in.) Few objects possess the magick and mystery of the sword.

The Sword in History

While the sword is lionized today, that hasn't always been the case. The history of the sword is much more recent than that of the knife. Much of that is because the sword is a far more advanced piece of technology. A sword made of bone or stone is impractical because it will break in short order. Wooden swords are more durable, but they quickly lose their edge. Swords truly require metal, and to be truly effective, they need to be made of iron, and better yet, steel.

Today we think of spears as primitive weapons, but in the ancient world they were a primary weapon. The pottery of the ancient Greeks, for instance, depicts a whole lot of spears and very little in the way of swords. Certainly there were a lot of soldiers who carried swords, but those swords were very much a secondary weapon. Even the Romans primarily used the spear for much of their history, generally because sword technology was still rather limited. Early swords were made of bronze, a metal alloy consisting primarily of copper and tin. Bronze swords were eventually replaced with swords made of iron.

Bronze and iron are both so important in the development of human civilization that they have ages named after them. Bronze Age cultures existed from 3300 BCE and up until 600 BCE in parts of Europe. The Iron Age began as early as 1200 BCE in some places and lasted until 700 CE in others. The terms Bronze Age and Iron Age are problematic because every civilization had its own individual Bronze and/or Iron Age. Just because iron was being used in Rome doesn't mean it was being used in Germany. In Europe, the Iron Age ended in the year 1 CE, the beginning of the modern era, or Common Era (CE).

The ancient Greece of mythology and Homer's *Odyssey* is a Bronze Age culture, and swords from the period are common in museums and can even be purchased by private collectors. Bronze swords were sharp and mostly durable, but bronze just wasn't strong enough to make the sword a primary weapon. Swords in battle often bent, which was not ideal in combat. There are humorous stories of bronze weapons having to be straightened out on the battlefield; it's no wonder spears held sway for such a long period of time.

Early iron swords weren't much better than bronze. While they didn't bend as much, they often were brittle and were more likely to shatter. As technology improved, so did the sword, and eventually the Romans were able to manufacture quality steel swords like the *gladius*. The gladius was a strong short-sword that was an effective tool for both stabbing and hacking.

The sword as we generally think of it today came of age during the (European) Middle Ages (500–1500 CE). Utilizing technology borrowed from the Middle East, European blacksmiths began making high-quality swords. When we think of swords, we tend to think of knights, and that's because the sword rose to prominence during the Age of Chivalry, where it became immortalized in history, myth, and legend.

Swords in Mythology and History

Swords existed in mythology before the Middle Ages, but on a much more limited basis. Greek and Roman mythology is full of heroes, but they didn't wield swords like Excalibur. The most famous sword in Greek mythology is famous not because it was wielded by a brave warrior but because it became a popular metaphorical expression.

The *Sword of Damocles* was the name given to a sword suspended by a single horsehair over the throne of the Sicilian tyrant-king Dionysius II. In order to prove to the philosopher

Damocles just how difficult ruling was, Dionysius allegedly offered Damocles his throne. But the throne came with one caveat: a sword suspended over the philosopher's head. The sword served as a constant reminder of just how difficult rule could be, and that the rich and powerful often face problems that are overlooked by those envious of their status.

In Greek myth, the hero Theseus comes of age by moving a large rock and taking up his father's sword and sandals. In this case, Theseus's father is Aegeus, the king of Athens, and the sword signifies his heir-in-waiting status relative to the city-state's throne. Due to their rarity, swords in Bronze Age Greece conferred status. Theseus later used his father's sword to kill the dreaded and legendary Minotaur.

Though the sword features in Greek and Roman myth periodically, it reached legendary status in the myths of the Middle Ages. The sword features prominently in the myths of King Arthur, along with the Welsh and Irish myths that preceded and influenced the stories of the Knights of the Round Table. Norse and Anglo-Saxon myths also reference the sword. Many of the most popular and legendary figures of the Middle Ages possessed magical swords.

Excalibur is probably the most celebrated sword in all of mythology, but its history is a bit more tangled than most people realize. There are even two different versions of how Arthur obtained his legendary sword. The best-known version is "the sword in the stone" tale, where only the true king of the Britons can remove Excalibur from a large rock. Originally the sword was encased in an anvil, before being changed into a stone in later versions of the tale.

In the story of King Arthur, Excalibur represents justice, and the rock it was drawn from is symbolic of Jesus Christ. By pulling a sword of justice from a stone representing Christ, Arthur establishes himself as a king by divine right.[19] In some versions of this story, it's the knight Sir Galahad who removes a sword from a stone in preparation for his quest for the Holy Grail.

In the more magical version of how Arthur received Excalibur, he's given his sword by the mysterious Lady of the Lake on the Isle of Avalon. In that version, a hand breaks the surface of the lake and throws Excalibur and its scabbard to him. While Excalibur established Arthur as king, it was the sword's scabbard that was truly magical. The scabbard was said to protect its wearer from physical harm, but that bit of magick just doesn't capture the imagination like a powerful, shiny sword. Celtic swords were often more magical than the swords in other mythologies, with some even capable of song during battle!

Ties between Celtic myth and the stories of King Arthur are tedious at best, but Excalibur has several parallels in Welsh

---

19 Norris J. Lacy, ed., *The Arthurian Encyclopedia* (New York: Garland Publishing, 1986), p. 536.

mythology. The swords *Caladbolg* and *Caledfwich* are often compared to Arthur's legendary blade, with the latter even appearing in both Celtic and Arthurian tales.

Norse mythology is full of swords, though none of them are quite as famous as Thor's hammer, *Mjölnir*. (Curiously, in some version of Thor's myth, Mjölnir isn't a hammer at all, but an ax, another weapon with a sharp blade.) Swords in Viking mythology were generally prized for their strength and not their magical properties, though any sword capable of killing a dragon would have to have been infused with some degree of magick.

The creation of a sword was often seen as a magical event, and sometimes the smiths who forged famous swords became just as legendary as the heroes who wielded them. The most famous smith in all of European mythology is probably the Anglo-Saxon/Norse Wayland (often spelled Waland and sometimes Wieland), whose legend existed across Europe. Wayland has been known to show up in the mythology of the Franks, Anglo-Saxons, and the Norse and is still a popular figure in modern fantasy literature.

Wayland was more than a smith; in some myths he was also the Lord of the Elves! His legend was so powerful that he made swords for more than just gods and heroes; several historical figures also have swords attributed to Wayland. *Durendal*, the sword of Roland, nephew of the emperor Charlemagne, was

The Sword

said to have been made by the legendary smith. Wayland also shows up in the Norse *Edda* and the Anglo-Saxon poem *Beowulf*.

Famous swords weren't just reserved for mythological and pagan figures. In Islamic tradition, Ali, the son-in-law of the Prophet Muhammad, wielded the legendary *Zulfiqar*. Ali's sword is one of the more unique swords in history and legend, and is often depicted as having two points (looking a lot like an open pair of scissors). Zulfigar was a gift either from Muhammad or from the angel Gabriel.

In Christian tradition, a whole host of famous personages have had famous swords. The Frankish Emperor Charlemagne wore *Joyeuse* at his side, a sword so special it was said to shine brighter than even the sun. Eventually French kings used a sword purported to be Joyeuse at their coronation ceremonies.

The two most popular figures in Christian tradition after Jesus himself are both associated with the sword. The Apostle Peter actively used a sword in the New Testament, cutting off the ear of a servant (or slave) named Malchus. That sword allegedly still exists at a basilica in Poland (scholars today believe it to be a medieval forgery). The Apostle Paul is the "saint of swordsmen," and his symbol in the Roman Catholic Church is a sword positioned in front of a book.

The *Wallace Sword*, said to belong to the legendary Scottish freedom fighter William Wallace, is currently on display at the national monument that bears his name. It's unlikely that the sword actually belonged to the character depicted in the movie *Braveheart* because it's just too big. It's a two-handed sword with a blade over five feet long! To effectively wield what is today known as the Wallace Sword, Sir William would have had to have been unusually tall for his era.

Not only did the sword rule the Middle Ages, but it seems to rule the modern-day world as well. In fact, swords might be more popular today than they were a thousand years ago. They show up in books and are also part of several movie and video game franchises.

The Harry Potter series is probably best known for its use of the wand, but it makes room for blades as well. The *Sword of Gryffindor* plays a large role in J. K. Rowling's story, and Harry (along with his friends Ron Weasley and Neville Longbottom) uses the sword several times along his way to defeating the evil Lord Voldemort. The wands in Harry Potter are certainly cool, but I'd much rather have that Gryffindor sword!

We don't usually associate science fiction with swords, but they often show up there anyway. The most famous sword style of the last thirty-five years might be the lightsaber. It's no coincidence that Jedi "Knights" wield a weapon that looks remarkably similar to a sword. Blasters might be practical, but they lack the romance of a blade. My favorite sword duels are just as likely to involve Darth Maul, Luke Skywalker, and Yoda as they are King Arthur.

With over fifty million units sold, the *Legend of Zelda* video game franchise is one of the biggest in the industry. Central to the game is the *Master Sword* (or *Skyward Sword*) utilized by Zelda's hero, Link. In the *Super Smash Brothers* spinoff, Link's weapon of choice is also the sword. *Zelda* isn't the only series of video games to use swords; the weapon is central to games like *Dragon Quest* and entire online universes like that found in *World of Warcraft*.

J. R. R. Tolkien's Middle-Earth is home to several famous swords. The most famous is probably the glowing-blue *Sting* first used by Bilbo Baggins in *The Hobbit* and then later by his nephew Frodo in the Lord of the Rings trilogy. More powerful than Sting was Gandalf's *Glamdring*, which glowed white when in the presence of orcs. The sword *Andúril*, wielded by the hero Aragorn, was capable of stabbing both the living and the dead, and, just like Excalibur, indicated kingship.

In the series Percy Jackson and the Olympians, the protagonist (Percy Jackson, of course) also wields a sword. Since swords are pretty cumbersome and don't fit in your pocket, Jackson's sword *Riptide* turns into a pen when he's not using it. Author Rick Riordan's Jackson books are introducing a whole new audience to the Greek gods, and there's no better way to introduce people to that mythology than with the sword as your hero's primary weapon.

High fantasy has turned into big business since the release of the Harry Potter and the Lord of the Rings movies, and that means we are only going to see more swords in the future. No other weapon in history has been as romanticized as the sword, and I'm reminded of that every time I see the Witch's circle cast with one.

Sword Lore

The sword has long been a symbol of royal power, and this has continued into the present day. When a new king or queen is crowned in Great Britain, there are five different swords used in the coronation ceremony. All five swords are also considered part of the United Kingdom's "Crown Jewels." One of those swords, the *Curtana* (or *Sword of Mercy*), dates back to the thirteenth century, and the largest sword in the collection, the *Great Sword of State*, is used annually to open Parliament.

Beginning in the Middle Ages, Christians used to swear and take oaths on a sword most likely because it resembles a cross. Those who swore on a sword generally did so at the intersection of the guard and hilt, the most cross-like part of any sword. For Witches, this is all of little consequence, but the image of a knight kneeling on one knee in front of a sword, with his hands on the top of his sword, is one that is recognizable in all sorts of mythology and literature.

Perhaps due to their rather aggressive and masculine energy, swords have been involved in several different courtship rites throughout the centuries. Prospective grooms who were lucky and rich enough to own a sword in the Middle Ages and into the Renaissance often popped the question by presenting a wedding ring on their sword's hilt. No doubt the sword hinted at the groom's virility and strength.

Even more virile is a Norwegian tradition that involves the groom plunging a sword into the ceiling beam of a house. A good strike guaranteed a productive and successful marriage, and a bad one was seen as a sign of potential trouble and, more quietly, future impotence on the part of the groom. This tradition lasted into the eighteenth century, so it's not all that far removed from the modern world.

While swords were certainly seen as symbols of masculinity and power, they also had the power to prevent copulation. In the legend of Tristan and Iseult (dating back to the eleventh and twelfth centuries), the couple is sometimes cleared of the crime of premarital sex because they kept a sword between them while sleeping. The idea that a sword might prevent a couple from making love is present in several Western cultures. The idea is found among the Norse and Arabic as well as the French and Irish sources that inspired the stories of Tristan and Iseult.

In Taoism, swords are used to cleanse and purify altars, ridding them of negative energies. Because swords are so beloved and honored by many Taoists, China has a great deal of sword folklore. It's considered bad luck, for instance, to place a sword on the ground or partially unsheathe a blade. When someone offers a blade to you, it's considered proper form (and good luck) to accept the sword with both hands.

In China and Japan, swords are thought to have something akin to souls, and as such people often honor them with offerings. Gifts such as flowers or scented oils will draw good spirits and energies into your sword, while gifts of blood or red meat will draw more negative entities. In some Eastern traditions, it's important to give your sword an offering so it won't turn on the one wielding it.

I'm not sure that there's a spirit hiding in my sword, but there is a lot of energy. Much like my athames, I think that my sword has a definite personality, and the more I think about it, a gift or offering to my sword is probably a good idea. It certainly couldn't hurt!

Blessing a Sword for Coven Work or Group Ritual

Swords are one of the few working tools often shared by an entire coven. Because of the sword's unique nature, a group blessing can help every covener take a small bit of ownership in a shared group sword

Before blessing the coven sword, make sure it's properly consecrated. The consecration ritual in chapter 4 of this book is a great place to start. The consecration and group blessing of the coven sword can be done back to back or over the course of a few gatherings. The best lunar phase for tool consecration is the new moon, as it symbolizes and empowers new beginnings. For blessings, a moon of abundance is the best choice, with the full moon (or time around the full moon) being optimal. Sometimes waiting for lunar phases isn't practical, but when you can do so, I think it adds a little extra oomph to the rites.

This particular blessing is designed to do two things for the sword and those in the coven:

1. *Familiarize everyone in the coven with the sword's own unique energies and introduce the sword to the energies of everyone in the coven.* We all make introductions to those individuals with whom we practice the Craft, so why not also introduce ourselves to the tools we will be using?

2. *Give everyone in the coven a bit of ownership in the sword.* Unless your coveners have all chipped in together to buy a new sword, it's likely that the coven sword has one individual owner who is allowing the whole coven to borrow it, so to speak. In my own coven, that's our situation. Our sword is technically mine, but I want everyone I circle with to feel a bit of an attachment to it. It's a very important tool in ritual—it's what takes us between the worlds! That's a pretty big deal, and I want my covenmates to know that as long as we are performing ritual together, the sword is also "theirs."

At the start of the blessing rite, the sword should be in the hands of the coven's ritual leader. She should begin by slowly walking around the circle deosil (clockwise), with the sword stretched out before her almost as if she was in the process of casting a magick circle. As she walks, everyone in the coven should take a few moments to really look at the coven sword. They should notice its newness, or in some cases, the wear and tear it has endured over the years, decades, or centuries. Those looking should reach out to the sword with all their senses to see if they can detect a bit of its history or energy.

As she walks around the circle, the high priestess should make some remarks about the coven sword and the role it plays in the coven.

> *With this sword we travel between the worlds. It is our gateway into a time that is not a time and to a place that is not a place. This sword is our gateway to the lands where both gods and mortals dwell. Because this sword transports all of us in this coven to that magical realm, it's important that we all feel an attachment to it, that we all know this sword, and that it knows us.*

The priestess should now return to her customary place in the circle. Once there, she should hold the sword out and away from her body horizontally, with one hand on the hilt and another on the blade. (She should do this if the blade is not sharp. If it is sharp, the sword should be held vertically with the point facing downward.) Holding the sword comfortably but with power and authority, she should say:

This sword was born in fire, and tonight it is blessed and reborn in service to this coven! One by one we shall bless our coven sword and share with it our energy. By doing so, it will better recognize those who stand here and better work with our own energies.

The priestess should now slowly tip the sword downward so that its point lightly touches the floor. When the sword is in the proper place, she should continue:

When the sword is passed to you, slowly lower the point to the floor and then push a bit of your own energy inside of it. Feel the energy flow from you down through your hands and into the hilt and then the blade. Be sensitive to that energy as it descends down the blade. When you feel it reach the point of the sword, open yourself up to the sword's energy and feel it travel up the length of the blade until that power touches the hilt and then you. Once the energy has returned to you, speak a truth about how our sword will be used in ritual.

The sword should be slowly raised off the floor and then handed horizontally to the coven member on the priestess's left, the sword now moving around the circle deosil. Coveners can say whatever they wish after exchanging energy with the sword, but here are a few ideas:

With this blade we shall walk between the worlds.

This sword is our gateway to the mysteries.

With steel and iron at our side, we shall be safe in this circle from all that would wish us harm.

This is the key that shall unlock the magick of the Lady and the Lord.

To journeys past and the journeys that await.

In perfect love and perfect trust we walk this path together.

Thou art an entryway to the land of spirit.

May this sword always lead us toward love, joy, and truth.

From this blade, power and wisdom.

May this sword always be a light that will help to return us all home to this coven.

A shield against all wickedness and evil.

May this sword assist in the work
and legacy of this coven.

Together we share this sword, and it a bit of us.

Once the sword has been passed around the coven and returned to the high priestess, she should hold it over the center of the altar and instruct everyone to gather around it. Once the coven has been gathered, everyone but the high priestess (who is holding the sword) should hold their middle and index fingers to their lips and share a kiss with the sword. (Fingers should be kissed and then brought down to the sword.)

With everyone touching the sword, the priestess says:

Together we have blessed this sword that it might better serve our coven. In perfect love and perfect trust we close this rite with the words: so mote it be! (*So mote it be!* is repeated by the coven.)

The sword has now been blessed and should be returned to its customary place on the altar until it is used to release the circle.

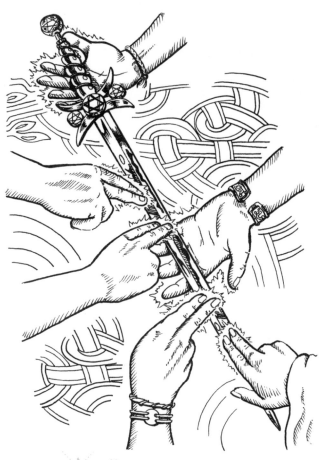

*Many hands touching a sword
as a form of blessing*

The Sword

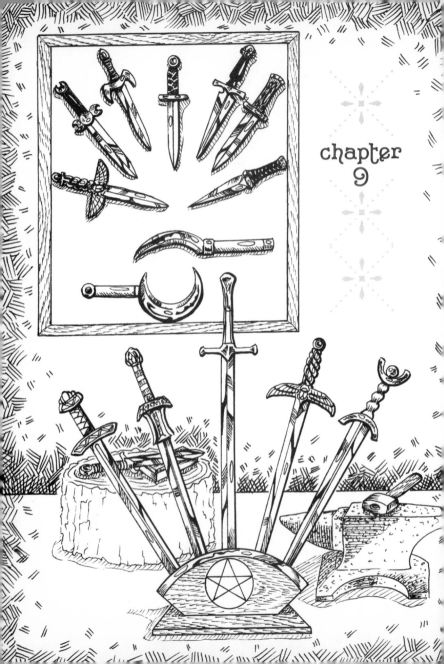

Divination, Ritual, and Spellwork with the Athame

Witches have been associated with prophecy and fortunetelling for thousands of years. The Witches in Shakespeare's *Macbeth* foretold the future, and countless Witches in the present day read tarot cards, tea leaves, and anything else that might provide a glimpse of the future. Though the athame is not generally thought of as a divination tool, it can be used as such, and often with great results.

Scrying with an Athame

Scrying is an ancient art and is generally used for catching glimpses of the future. Most people who scry use an external focus, generally a mirror, but anything reflective can be used for scrying. It's not possible to scry with every athame. You'll need one with a reflective surface, with the best results generally coming from blades made of stainless steel or polished stone.

Unlike other forms of scrying, when you scry with your athame you won't catch glimpses of the future, but just bits of your true path. You should scry with the athame when you aren't sure of the direction in your life or are unable to determine your heart's content. Here are some of the questions I've asked my athame over the years:

Am I truly in love with this person or just infatuated?

What project should I be working on?

Where is all the stress in my life coming from?

Am I on the right spiritual path for me?

I use my athame to answer questions about myself. I would never use my athame to scry for anyone else.

Since the athame is an extension of each individual Witch, it's especially suited for revealing one's true will. Few other tools are as attached to the individual Witch as the athame, so what tool could be better for delving into the psyche of a Witch? When used as a scrying device, the athame allows us to look inward and see our deepest desires.

When I scry with my athame, I usually set up a small altar near a window if it's a night of the full moon. If the moon is not very bright, I'm less choosy about where I set up, but I do try to make myself comfortable. If I use a kneeling altar, I provide pillows for my knees or use a chair. I like to reflect moonlight off my blade if possible, but candlelight works just as well. I find that setting my athame on a black cloth (or other dark-colored material) helps me focus better. Burning a little incense also sometimes helps create a magical mood. Make sure to polish your athame before this ritual so it's as reflective as possible.

After you've set up your altar area, you'll want to charge the athame with some of your own personal power. Drop most of your conscious thought for a few moments and then direct your gaze inward. Eventually you should try to focus on a brightly burning fire inside of yourself, which is representative of your true will. I always picture this near my heart. Gaze upon that fire for a minute or two and take a deep breath. Now feel that burning energy move through your body, along your arm, and eventually into your blade. "Push" the energy into your athame so that your blade radiates with your will and power.

After the blade is sufficiently charged, raise it above your head, perhaps holding it out toward the moon if it is full, and say:

> *Lord and Lady, I come this night to ask a boon.*
> *By powers of earth, air, fire, water, sun, and moon,*

Divination, Ritual, and Spellwork with the Athame

I seek to see my right path and know my true will.
Athame, reveal the answers with truth and skill.
So mote it be!

Set the athame down on your black cloth and make sure to position it in such a way that there's light reflecting off of it. You should also be able to make out a bit of your face in the blade. I always try to focus on capturing my eyes on the reflective surface of my athame. The idea that the eyes are the gateway to the soul is an old one and feels like good magical advice.

After your blade has been positioned, you'll want to verbalize your question. It's important here to be as specific as possible. If you don't want a vague answer, don't ask a vague question.

Once you've asked the question, stare into the blade of your athame. Let your eyes lose focus, and clear your mind of as many thoughts as possible. If you find yourself thinking anything, let it be the question you are asking. I sometimes find myself trying to "look past" the reflection of my eyes on the athame's blade. It's beyond our physical selves where we will be able to find the answers we seek. Sometimes I see what look like storm clouds rolling across my athame and then parting right before I see the answer I'm seeking.

I don't always "see" the answers to my questions on the steel of my blade; there have been times when it's more like a feeling. If I find myself not getting an answer after a substantial period of time, I touch one index finger to the pommel and the other to the knife's point, then close my eyes and look inward. At that point I've probably ceased actually "scrying," but I find that the flow of energy from the athame into myself and back again is a good source for drawing out an answer.

Answers while scrying can come in many forms. For some people it's a very real vision; for others it's a sudden determination that there's one particular path that's right for them. When I scry with the athame, I often find myself becoming sure of a particular decision. It's almost as if a seed in my brain has suddenly sprouted and grown about a foot in just a few minutes.

If you find yourself not getting an answer, that's okay. There are times when even our true selves struggle to figure out what path we should be walking. When there's no answer, set aside your question for a few days and try not to struggle with it. Let your subconscious mind work on the problem; answers often appear when we aren't obsessing over them. After a week or so, try scrying with your athame again and the answer might just reveal itself.

When you are done with your scrying ritual, be sure to thank the gods for any wisdom you might have received. If your question wasn't answered, still thank the gods; it's best to keep them on your side. A quick kiss to your blade as a thank-you is a good idea too.

The Athame Pendulum

One of the easiest forms of divination is the use of a pendulum. All that's required to make a pendulum is generally a stone or crystal and a small length of string or chain. When divining with a pendulum, the Witch simply holds the pendulum, waits for it to swing, and then determines the answer based either on the swinging motion or the final area the pendulum points to after moving. I usually use the pendulum for yes/no questions, but if you find yourself proficient with its use, it can be used to answer more involved questions as well.

One of the great advantages of using your athame as a pendulum is that it doesn't require any extra work. Unlike a store-bought pendulum or even a freshly minted stone/crystal pendulum, your athame has already been blessed and consecrated, and it knows you better than nearly any other tool on your working altar. You don't have to take any extra time getting to know your pendulum because you already know it. Your athame is seeped in your energy and power and wants to work with you.

Since your athame responds directly to your magical will, it's well suited for divination. The questioning energy coming out of you will generally cause your blade to swing just a little bit, enough to provide you with an answer. Because most athames are in tune with their owners, the athame pendulum is best at answering personal questions. I don't use it to answer questions for friends, family members, or covenmates.

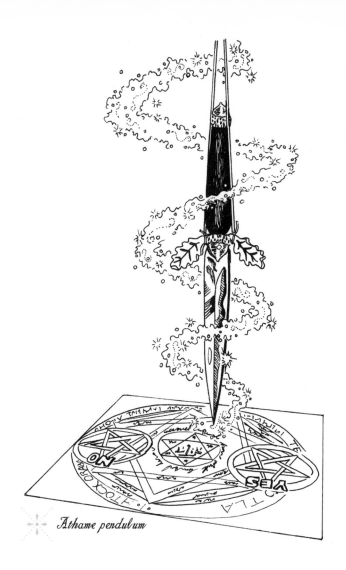

Athame pendulum

195

Divination, Ritual, and Spellwork with the Athame

When using your athame as a pendulum, it's important to make sure that it's reasonably well balanced. Simply tying a piece of string around the pommel will give your pendulum a very pronounced tilt, resulting in it continually favoring one side. An easy work-around for this is to use two pieces of string, tying each one to where the crossguard meets your knife's handle. If you then hold on to the two pieces of string right above your knife's pommel, the pendulum should balance pretty easily.

To use your pendulum with a minimum of fuss, you'll need to decide what its movements mean. The best way to do this is by asking your pendulum questions you already know the answers to. You could ask the pendulum a question such as "Am I twenty-four years old?" If you are twenty-four years old and it moves to the left, then movement toward the left implies "yes." If it moves to the right and you aren't twenty-four, then rightward movement means "no." I usually ask three to four questions here to make sure I've got my yes/no responses figured out properly.

I generally place a board with some already printed-out answers under my pendulum to get a clearer reading. This also allows the individual Witch to add a few other categories beyond yes or no. The most common other answers are generally "ask again" and "answer unclear." Receiving "ask again" as an answer is often a sign that your question was asked improperly. It's possible that you didn't put enough of your own energy into the question or that you asked the question in such a vague way that no answer was possible. Responses like "answer unclear" generally imply that there are currently too many variables involved to provide a proper answer. Sometimes restating the question helps, but other times it's best to put the pendulum away and ask again in a few days.

Pendulum boards are often made in the shape of a pentagram, but any shape that appeals to the individual Witch is acceptable. Some Witches go so far as to fill their pendulum boards with letters and numbers, like a Ouija board. That amount of information feels like overkill to me, and if I wanted such an involved answer, I'd probably pull out a deck of tarot cards. With the pendulum, simple is always best.

I use a pendulum for quick answers, meaning I generally skimp on the ceremony. Before asking a question, I usually ask the Lord and the Lady to guide my endeavors, but other than that, there's very little pomp and circumstance. If you have a lot of questions you need answers to, then I suggest a little extra ritual: light some incense, play some music, and maybe even cast a magick circle if you feel the need. Of course, if your need for divination is that great, you might want to use a technique a bit more advanced than the pendulum.

Divination, Ritual, and Spellwork with the Athame

Candle Carvings

When working as a solo Witch, my go-to spells generally involve candle magick. Candles provide an effective and easy way to work magick, and the athame (or white-handled knife, depending on your preference) can play a large role in that work. As an instrument of our will, the athame is uniquely suited to aiding our magical undertakings.

Candle magick really requires only two things: a candle and something with which to light that candle. The simplest way to prepare a candle for spellwork is to hold it in your hand and pour your intent into it. If you are trying to get a new job, simply focus on the type of job you want and see yourself happy and fulfilled within it. Then take that energy and pour it into the candle. When the candle is lit, that energy will then go out into the universe and hopefully give you your desired outcome.

That's the simplest way to use candle magick, but not necessarily the most effective way. The longer you work on something like a candle, the more will and emotion you put into it. It's also important to focus on exactly what you want. That's one of the things about magick: you often get what you ask for, but what you get is not always quite what you were expecting. When I was an angsty college student, I did a few love spells, and they generally worked. I'd fall pretty hard for somebody, but I always forgot to ask for that emotion to be reciprocated. Specifics matter, and that's one of the reasons the athame can be such a help when doing candle magick. Since the athame is a conduit for our true will, it's sometimes better at harnessing our true intentions than we are.

I usually start any candle spell by writing out my intention on an index card. From there I move on to dressing my candle with oil. There's no right or wrong kind when it comes to oil; simply use a type of oil that you believe relates to what you are trying to achieve. If you are trying to draw something to you (like love or money), anoint the candle from the bottom up. If you are trying to remove something (like a bad habit), anoint it downward, starting at the wick.

After the anointing is where the athame comes in. There are several different ways to carve on a candle, and they are all correct. The easiest is to write out whatever you are trying to achieve directly on the candle in plain English. Carving into a candle with a knife requires a large degree of concentration and skill, even though it sounds simple. It's even trickier if your knife is sharp on the edges. Etching out a *T* is pretty easy, but an *S*, much less so.

A more complicated method of candle carving involves the use of magical alphabets (like the Norse runes or Theban script—see the appendices). Magical alphabets are effective tools in magick because they require extra concentration. The longer you work on a candle, the more powerful it will be. Using a bunch of symbols that you are not overly familiar with requires extra work—and more time devoted to your candle. The figures in those alphabets are also a bit trickier to carve, requiring extra attention to detail.

No matter what alphabet I use when writing on a candle, I generally add a few extra "Witch marks" when I'm done. I always ask for the blessings of the Lord and the Lady in whatever magical endeavor I'm undertaking, so I like to put their symbols on my candles (see the illustration of Witch symbols in chapter 3). I also like to use phrase "the power going forth," because it's representative of my candle's intended purpose.

There's a third type of carving that I like to do, which I think of as "letting my intentions go free." Instead of concentrating on a specific alphabet, I shut off my mind and use my athame as a conduit for my true will. I allow the athame, my unconscious mind, and my hand to draw whatever on my candle. Usually I end up with a lot of random squiggles and other things, but those random squiggles represent what's inside of me. When I have trouble expressing my problems or needs, I turn off my active mind and trust that my true will and my athame will know what needs to be done to help fix the situation.

Out of all of our tools, it's the athame that we use to direct our power and energy. What wouldn't we want to use it in our magical endeavors? It's a precise way to infuse whatever we are doing with our magical energy. It's easy enough to use a sewing pin to mark on a candle, but does that pin know us like our athame does? Do we cast circles with such items or salute the elements with them? No, and that's what makes the athame so effective when it's used to carve on a candle.

After my intent and words have been poured into my candle via the athame, I like to charge the candle in my hands before lighting it. If I've got time to spare, I might leave the candle on my altar for a few days and wait for the appropriate lunar phase before releasing the power contained within it. (This also allows the candle to soak up a little bit more of my energy before the spell is finalized.) It's not necessary to wait for a waxing or full moon to do a prosperity spell, but it can be helpful if you're not in a big hurry.

When I actually get to the point of burning the candle, I like to put underneath it my original notecard denoting the candle's purpose. When lighting the candle, I usually ask the gods to bless my work with a quick little prayer:

> *Lord and Lady, bless the work that I do here this night.*
> *May my magick powerfully flow from*
> *candle's light. So mote it be!*

The spell is generally finished when the candle has finished burning or has reached a specific endpoint specified by the Witch.

For my own spells, I sometimes end up using long taper candles. Long tapers are great because they emit a powerful flame and allow for lots of carving room. However, they take a long time to burn out completely. Since a candle should never be left unattended and I don't always have the time necessary to wait for a candle to burn down completely, I sometimes mark a specific spot on the candle where all of its energy shall be released.

Some Witches marks such spots by sticking a needle into the candle, with the spell's energy released when the candle burns down to the pin. That's certainly an effective way to mark the end of a spell, but there's an even easier way. Using the athame, simply draw a circle around the spot in the candle where you want the spell to end. I generally don't mark anything above a quarter of the way down the candle's length; I usually settle for a circle in the middle of the candle.

It's important to do more than just draw a circle on the candle; the circle that's being created has to forcefully represent your intent. While drawing the circle, I usually reflect on its purpose internally while stating my intention out loud:

At this line my magick shall be unleashed.
All this candle's energy will be released. So mote it be!

When you are done with the spell, it's customary to bury the candle you've used or to melt down what's left of it to create a new candle. If I'm using a long taper and have a lot of it left over, I'll sometimes choose to honor the candle by placing it somewhere in my ritual room and letting its remaining light illuminate my other workings until it burns out completely.

Spell to Let Go of a Lover or Friend

We all have moments when we realize that we need to move on from a lover or friend. Sometimes it's simply because a relationship didn't quite work out, and sometimes it's because our "friends" put us in a compromising or dangerous situation. Most Witches follow the dictate of the Wiccan Rede, which states, "An it harm none, do what you will." It's a rule I follow with every bit of magick I practice; however, sometimes circumstances call for extremely proactive spellwork. This is a spell of that nature.

This is a simple spell that requires only some string, two objects you can tie together (I suggest something like popsicle sticks), and your athame. Start by deciding which one of the two items to be tied together will represent you and which will represent a person in your life whom you need to let go of. Then hold the object representing you in your hands for a few moments and reflect on why it's time to end the relationship with the person you are letting go of. Picture yourself happy, healthy, and moving on with your life. Pour that energy into the item that's representing you.

Now take your athame and carve your name (or initials) into the object. You can also carve some additional things onto your item, such as runes of protection and/or strength (see appendix 2). Symbols of the gods are also appropriate here. What's important is that anything you draw on the object representing you really does reflect who you are and why you've come to this point in your life.

You could certainly use a marker for this part of the spell, or scratch into your item with wood, but the athame simply projects energy better. You want your emotions to be a part of your magical practice, and you want to infuse the items you do magick with to contain your energy. There's no better way to do that than with an athame.

The second stage of the spell is the most difficult and emotionally wrenching. Hold the second stick (or whatever item you use) in your hands and reflect on the person you are removing from your life. Think about the things that have brought you to this point, and reaffirm in your mind why this needs to be done. Hold the person's image in your mind's eye and feel it travel down your body and through your shoulders, your arms, and then finally the object in your hands.

Now carve the initials or the name of the person you wish to remove from your life on the second stick with the athame. If there are some symbols you wish to add, go ahead, but be sure to mind the Wiccan Rede while doing so. You may want to use a rune representing new beginnings for the person you are leaving behind, because in some ways they'll be starting a new chapter in their lives—a chapter you'll be free from!

If you want to add a little extra juice to this spell, you can add a few personal effects/items to the two items you will be tying together. In many Witch traditions a "personal effect" is often a lock of hair or a fingernail, but those sorts of things can be hard to come by. You can add a picture to each stick if you want, but with the initials/names carved on each item it shouldn't be necessary.

Now wrap your cord around the two items several times and tie them together while saying:

> *Once bound together,*
> *I remove this tether.*
> *The cord that bound*
> *Will soon be unwound.*

After you tie the items together, make sure that the object representing you is on top when you set them down. This is an expression of your power, as you are the one making this change to your lives.

Before cutting the cord binding the two of you together, state your intent to the universe:

> *Tonight I break the bonds that hold me to _____*
> *(person's name). Our time together is now at*
> *an end. With harm to none I cut these cords!*

Now cut the cord holding your two items together. As you move your athame through the cord, imagine the threads that once connected the two of you being removed. There's an old adage in Witchcraft that says "as above, so below," and truer words were never spoken in this case. With every piece of cut cord, you will be removing a tie that binds you to the person in question. I find cutting and reading at the same time to be dangerous, but if you want to say a few words while enacting your spell, here is a little incantation:

> *With one cut this love's undone.*
> *I rid myself of the harm you do.*
> *This thread is now broken.*
> *So mote it be, this Witch has spoken!*

When you've finished the spell, bury the item representing the other person in the ground. If that's not an option, you can also throw it into a body of water like a stream or river if it's a natural stick/branch. It's also acceptable to burn the item, but unless the person is downright horrible, that seems a little extreme to me. You can also just throw the item into a garbage can. My wife suggests either burying the cord used in the spell or perhaps keeping it as a reminder of lessons learned.

Spirits and the Blade

Gerald Gardner once described the athame as "the true Witch's weapon." This description has always been a bit troubling to me because I've never seen any use for a "weapon" during Witch ritual. Well, except for that one time…

That particular night wasn't anything special. The coven was practicing ritual as usual and we had gotten to the "working" part of our rite. We were preparing to chant and dance as a way to raise energy when one of my covenmates snatched my athame off our altar. He then turned and stabbed into the air, yelling, "Away!" The rest of us stood there in shock as he continued to make a few movements with my knife before finally yelling, "Be gone!"

He then placed my athame back on our altar and explained that he had felt a negative presence pressing in on our circle and attempting to join our ritual. My athame was the one closest to him (and as a good friend, he knew I wouldn't mind him touching it) and he felt the need to act immediately. He was acting on impulse but made the right decision. The athame can be an effective tool against dark forces.

As a Witch, I'm not a big believer in the Devil, but I do believe that there are negative forces in the world. Often these are malevolent spirits (ghosts) or perhaps fey with a poor view of humanity. Magick circles attract spiritual energies, so it's not surprising that such entities might peek in on a Witch ritual. Usually they are content to simply watch at a distance, but in rare instances they seek to lash out. My friend was reacting to one of those instances.

During a spectral intrusion, the athame can be used two very different ways. The first (and best) way is to use your athame to "push" the entity. This is a lot like casting the circle: you are summoning magical energy and then releasing it through the athame. The energy then propels the spirit (or other force) outward and away. Usually after getting whacked with the energy of an athame, the presence in question will either leave or keep a respectful distance.

My friend's reaction was more visceral and less planned than a push of energy. He grabbed my blade and slashed, attempting to cut the presence at the edge of our circle. Now, one can't really "cut" an unseen force, but stabbing an athame into an unwanted spectral visitor will most likely disrupt it. I'm not sure if this hurts the spirit, but it probably doesn't feel all that good. After my friend stabbed our "visitor," it departed our circle and hasn't shown up since.

I am not suggesting that any Witch should go and seek dark forces so they can bash them with their athame. However, if you do find yourself in such a situation, an athame is a good object to have on hand. A Witch never goes looking for trouble, but when trouble does find them, they know how to take care of the situation.

A Dedication Ritual

One of the first steps on the path of the Witch is a dedication ritual. This can be done with a group, but is often solitary. My first dedication ritual occurred a year and a day after I discovered modern Witchcraft as an adult. It was a simple solo rite. I walked into a cornfield, took off my clothes, and then asked the Goddess and the God to watch over me on my new path. The ritual included here is a little more elaborate.

This ritual is designed to be done at night outdoors, but it can also be done indoors as long as there is a window handy. If done indoors, you'll also need a bowl or pot filled with earth (dirt) and one with water. The only tool required for this ritual is your athame, but if you prefer to work with a full altar or some candles, that's perfectly acceptable. I prefer to end all of my rituals with the simple feast of cakes and ale, but that's not absolutely necessary.

Start the ritual by preparing yourself for what's to come. Envision yourself as a Witch nestled in the embrace of the Goddess and the God. Picture yourself working magick, casting a circle with your athame, and calling the quarters. When you are settled, begin the ritual as you usually would. Cast the circle, call the elements, and invoke the Lord and the Lady and/or whatever deities are part of your personal practice.

Once the initial steps are all done, stop for a second to talk to the Goddess and the God. Speak about what you want out of the Craft and how it has called to you. Talk about the steps that have brought you to this night and this time. If you are closer to one deity than the other, make mention of that. At my dedication ritual, I asked the Horned God to be a larger part of my life, and he obliged!

Before the dedication rite begins, articulate what you are about to do:

> *Tonight I dedicate myself to the Old Ways, to the*
> *Craft of the Wise, to Witchcraft. With this step I link*
> *myself to all Witches past and present. With Goddess*
> *and God as my witnesses, I make this oath and*
> *promise to them that I shall live my life as a Witch,*
> *doing as I will while harming none. So mote it be!*

Start by holding your athame out from your body, being sensitive to the breeze. As the power of air touches you and your blade, say:

> *Her breath is the power to know. I dedicate myself to*
> *the mysteries of the Craft, the gods, and this world.*
> *May my journey ever be of knowledge. Blessed be!*

Now hold your athame up to the moon and reflect its light down upon you while saying:

Her reflection is the power to dare. I dedicate myself
to the known and the unknown. A Witch never walks
in fear. May my steps ever be confident. Blessed be!

Unless you live in a very dry part of the world, there should be some dew on the ground. If there is not, this next part can be done at any body of water or with a small bowl or chalice of water. Dip your blade into the water or wipe it upon the wet earth and say:

His touch is the power to will. I dedicate
myself to striding ever forward. There is no
obstacle that cannot be overcome. May my
path ever be one of progress. Blessed be!

Now finally take your athame and plunge it into the earth while saying:

His touch is the power to keep silent. I dedicate
myself to hearing the words of the Lord and the
Lady and my brothers and sisters in the Craft.
May my quest ever yield rewards. Blessed be!

With these four simple steps, you've invoked the Lord and the Lady and all the elements. Before ending the rite, stop to thank the Lord and the Lady:

I came to this place as just another person. I now
leave it as a dedicated Witch! As a Witch, I'm a
priestess (or priest) of the gods, a being of magick,
and one who walks hand in hand with the earth.
My will has led me to this place so that I might
walk between the worlds! I thank the Lord and the
Lady for guiding my path and the powers of the
elements for blessing me this night. So mote it be!

If you've brought along cakes and ale, this is a great time for a simple feast. When you are done eating and drinking, be sure to leave some behind as a thank-you to the gods, the fey who might be watching, the earth, and the elements. You are now a dedicated Witch!

An Initiation Ritual

As an instrument of one's true will, the athame fits nicely into the initiation rituals of a Witch. Initiations are typically done in covens to signify full acceptance of the rites and mysteries of a particular group. Initiation rituals figure prominently in many Witchcraft traditions, though any coven should feel free to start their own. Many initiated Witches can trace their lineage back seventy years or more, though age does not necessarily mean one tradition is better or greater than another.

The coven that meets at my house has only been together for a little over three years, and we have an initiation ritual. We have one because it draws the entire coven closer together, and a well-done initiation rite can be a life-changing event. There's something powerful about publicly proclaiming your love of the Craft and feeling the love of your coven members. I think it's an important rite, and I wish more covens made it an important part of their work.

Since this ritual was written with my coven in mind, the major players in it are the high priestess, the high priest, and the initiate. I work almost exclusively with my wife, which means we utilize the high priestess–high priest dynamic. For a ritual such as this, any combination of clergy is acceptable. Having two high priestesses (or priests) works just fine. I'm not a fan of "group" initiations. Every initiate should get their own ritual, though running through three or four of them in one evening is fine. Just make sure the focus of the high priestess rests exclusively on one initiate at a time.

For this ritual you will need some easy-to-cut cords. Cords are readily available at most fabric and hobby stores. Thick ropes of yarn will also work here and are probably even easier to cut. My wife and I prefer the color red for cords, though the color used is completely a matter of personal taste.

Initiation rituals generally require the use of two rooms or spaces. There should be a "sitting room" for initiates, along

Divination, Ritual, and Spellwork with the Athame

with the regular working space. I begin my coven's initiations by leading the future initiates into the sitting room. Once they are comfortable, I take their athames and put them on the altar where the ritual will occur.

While the initiate waits to be summoned, you should have them write a letter about what they hope to gain from the Craft over the following year. When they are done, they should seal it and place it in a secure space. Upon the anniversary of their initiation, give the letter back to them so they can see how far they've come over the past year.

The initiation rite begins like any other ritual. The altar is prepared, the circle is cast, the quarters are called, and the Lord and the Lady are invoked. To make the initiation circle a little more special, it's nice to lay it out both physically and spiritually. Before the ritual begins, create an actual circle in your working space. Using something as simple as white flour looks impressive here (and is easily swept up or vacuumed). Leaves, sand, flowers, and rocks are other options. A physical circle boundary is not necessary, but it will add tremendously to the ambiance.

Once the opening parts of the ritual are finished, the high priestess or high priest should go and collect the initiate, taking two cords with them. Upon reaching the initiate, the high priestess should ask them:

*Tonight you seek the Craft of the Wise and the Way
of the Witch. How do you approach the circle and
those who would share with you the mysteries?*

The initiate should respond with:

In perfect love and perfect trust.

Among the initiate and the initiators, there should always be "perfect love and perfect trust." Its more than just a phrase; it's the way of doing within a solid coven.

After the "password" has been said by the initiate, the high priestess should then instruct the initiate on what lies ahead:

*The path of the Witch is not for the faint of
heart. It's one full of peril, and yet its rewards
are sweeter than honey. You come to me with
perfect love and perfect trust, and I do to you,
yet now I would bound you before presenting you
to the gods. Do you accept this development?*

The initiate should respond with "yes" or some other affirmative comment.

The priestess then instructs the initiate to hold out their hands, dominant hand outward. When the hands have been presented, she takes the first cord and bounds them loosely at the wrists, saying:

We are often bound to the world of the mundane,
unable to see the true beauty and magick of
this world. This cord represents that tether to
the unmagickal, all that often holds us back
from walking the path of the Witch.

After the wrists are bound, the priestess loosely binds the initiate's feet together at the ankles. Special care should be taken here to make sure the initiate can still walk comfortably. The binding here is more symbolic than physical. While tying the ankles together, the priestess says to the initiate:

Only in free will can one truly live as a Witch. I
can initiate you into our coven's mysteries, but
the choice to walk our path lies with you. This
obstacle is one that only the individual Witch can
overcome. I may guide your steps this night, but
the journey that lies before you is truly your own.

The initiate is led slowly into the working space, the priestess making sure that the initiate does not trip on the cords. When the pair reaches the perimeter of the working space, the circle is opened with the athame and the high priestess and the initiate are allowed to enter. The high priest then provides one final warning:

*You are now preparing to enter a temple between
the worlds, a circle where both mortals and
gods dwell. Before you stands the path of the
Witch, behind you a normal existence free from
the responsibilities that come as a member
of the Craft. Do you wish to proceed?*

If the initiate replies in the affirmative, the ritual continues and all three participants move to stand before the altar.

The initiate is then instructed to kneel. Standing before the initiate, the high priestess takes the initiate's hands into her own and raises them into the air. She examines the initiate's hands while saying:

*So much of this world seeks to blind us from the
gods. The Witch knows that the divine exists
everywhere in this world. It exists in the forests,
the oceans, the rivers, and in our imaginations. It
exists wherever we feel love for this earth and our
sisters and brothers who walk upon it with us. By
removing this cord, I remove the blinders that keep
us from experiencing the true power of this world.*

The high priest looks at the initiate's hands being held by the high priestess and touches them briefly before continuing:

Divination, Ritual, and Spellwork with the Athame

*To experience that power and to escape that which
blinds us, every Witch should know the greatest
mystery. It is the foundation of all magick and
illustrates the divinity of this world. "As above,
so below" is the secret of the Witch. The power
to see and do all things resides both within and
without us. Now that you know the mystery,
do you wish to continue, knowing that how
you see the world will be forever changed?*

The initiate should reply in the affirmative.

Grabbing her athame off of the altar, the high priestess cuts the cord, freeing the hands of the initiate, while saying:

*I now remove all that separates you from the gods.
The Lord and the Lady exist in this place, and they
exist within you and me. As above, so below, indeed.*

The high priest now stands before the initiate and says:

*While we have removed the first obstacle keeping
you from the mysteries, the second obstacle is
one that you must remove yourself. You must
truly want to walk the path of the Witch.
You must set your feet upon that path.*

The high priestess picks up the initiate's athame from the altar and holds it out to them, saying:

*This is the athame, the true Witch's weapon. It
lies at the heart of our mysteries, for our mysteries
are those of the self. Those who wield the athame
wield their true will in the circle. Is it your will
to walk the path of the Witch with this coven?*

After the candidate replies with "yes," the priestess continues:

*Then take this blade and free yourself from what still
separates you from this coven, for you are the only one
who can set your own feet onto the path of the Craft.*

The initiate should feel free to sit on the ground to cut the cord around their feet. It's important that this last step is done safely. No one wants to end their initiation ceremony doubled over on the floor or falling onto the coven's altar. When both cords have been cut, they may be given to the initiate or placed in a jar with the cut cords of other coven members. The cords can also be burned if one wishes, as they symbolize obstacles.

Once the initiate is free of their restraints, they should stand before the priestess and priest, with one of them declaring the initiate a new member of the coven. If your coven uses magical names while in the circle, this is an excellent opportunity to ask the new initiate for their magical name. The high priestess or priest should then say:

Divination, Ritual, and Spellwork with the Athame

Let it now be known to the four watchtowers,
Spirit, the Great Goddess, and the Horned One that
(initiate's name or magical name) is now a member of
(coven name). We welcome them to our mysteries. So
mote it be!

(Everyone in the circle repeats, *So mote it be.*)

Still holding their athame, the new initiate is instructed to visit each of the four cardinal points and draw an invoking pentagram while announcing themselves to all four watchtowers:

Hail the element of air/fire/water/earth! Let it be
known to all the watchtowers that I, (Witch's name),
am a Witch of the (coven name). So mote it be!

After hailing all the watchtowers, the candidate then approaches the altar and speaks to the Lady and the Lord and/or the specific deities of the coven. There they hail the Goddess and the God and announce their name and that they are a Witch.

Hail the great Lady! Great Goddess, I have
received your mysteries and been initiated into
the (coven name). Tonight, I, (Witch's name),
have been accepted by my brothers and sisters
in the Craft as a true Witch. So mote it be!

After the Goddess has been addressed, the initiate addresses the Horned God:

> *Hail the true Lord! Horned One, I have received*
> *your mysteries and been initiated into the*
> *(coven name). Tonight, I, (Witch's name),*
> *have been accepted by my brothers and sisters*
> *in the Craft as a true Witch. So mote it be!*

The candidate now stands as a full member of the coven. In many traditions it's customary to celebrate with gifts and feasting after an initiation. If the coven is initiating several different individuals over the course of one night, each new member of the coven is allowed to stay in the circle and assist the high priestess and priest in any way they desire, or sit quietly and observe the next initiation.

Divination, Ritual, and Spellwork with the Athame

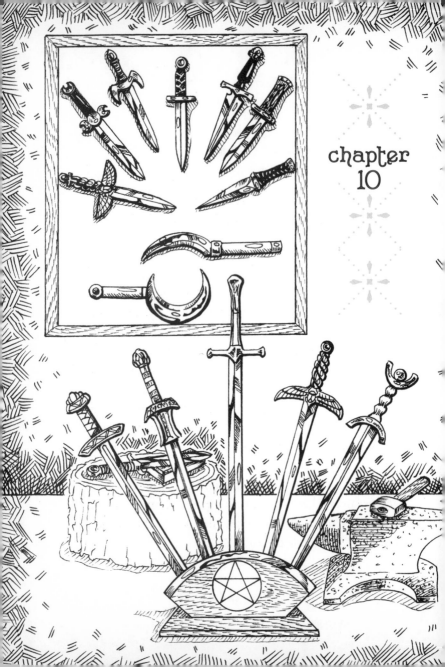

The Knife in
Traditional Witchcraft

There are many different types of Witchcraft in the Western world. The most common is Wicca, and the majority of the rituals and information in this book are Wiccan in nature, but that's not the whole story. In recent years there has been a surge of interest in what's known as *Traditional Witchcraft*, a tradition that also uses ceremonial blades.

Traditional Witchcraft is hard to define because there are several different competing definitions. There are all sorts of people who call themselves "Traditional Witches," and they don't all agree on what constitutes their tradition. Generally, Traditional Witches claim to utilize a body of knowledge different from that of Gerald Gardner and his later initiates. They also often claim that their tradition is older than the one revealed by Gardner in the early 1950s.

Oftentimes Traditional Witchcraft is influenced by *cunning craft*, a type of folk magick popular in Great Britain from the end of the Middle Ages right up until World War I. Cunning craft is a mixture of folk magick and information taken from books. Cunning folk were both men and women, and they provided a broad range of services. They were often employed to find lost items, heal the sick, and remove curses.

Today it's easy to think of those folks as "Witches," but that was not how they self-identified. Most practitioners of cunning craft were Christians and they were often called upon to remove spells and curses that people believed were cast onto them by witches. Cunning folk were occasionally persecuted for practicing magick, but were generally seen as just another part of the community. Some cunning men were even village priests!

Just like modern Witches, the cunning folk of the last five centuries used magical knives for a variety of purposes. Many of these tasks were mundane, but some were most certainly magical. The cunning folk used their knives to cut herbs for spells and potions and to carve symbols onto candles.

Many cunning folk also used their knives (and sometimes even a sword) to cast magick circles while hunting for buried treasure. The circles were important for treasure hunting because it was widely believed that ghosts or other such spirits guarded underground treasure hoards. The circle provided protection from the bad spirits and helped contribute to the idea that cunning folk often worked with the spirits of the dead. In that spirit many modern Traditional Witches work with spirits or ancestors.

Most cunning folk were literate and utilized magical texts such as the *Key of Solomon* to assist them in their magical endeavors. Those texts often required the use of a ritual dagger or knife. In magick both high and low, blades are nearly always present.

The most famous and influential Traditional Witch of the last sixty years was an Englishman named Roy Bowers (1931–1966), better known by his pen name, Robert Cochrane. Cochrane claimed that many members of his family had practiced a secret form of Witchcraft over the last four hundred years, and that he could trace his family's involvement in the Craft back to the sixteenth century. Cochrane's claims have never been substantiated, but the type of Witchcraft he practiced and inspired has been influential to many Witches. Cochrane's original circle was known as the *Clan of Tubal Cain*, and many of the groups who were inspired by him have this title in their names. (Tubal Cain was a master smith in Hebrew legend.)

Much of Cochrane's Craft was similar to other forms of Witchcraft popular in the 1960s, but there were differences too. He utilized a distinct working tool he called a *stang*, and it was often the centerpiece of his workings. Cochrane's stang was often a wooden stick with two prongs or horns on top of it. The base of the stang was often wrapped in iron.

Perhaps more important to our purposes (this is a book about pointy metal things) was Cochrane's other version of the stang. Most tools in Witchcraft can generally be found lying around one's house, and in the case of the stang, it could generally be found lying around the barn. Cochrane's other version of the stang was the common pitchfork, an item unlikely to attract much notice in agricultural communities (or those who do a lot of gardening today).

In Cochrane's version of Witchcraft, the stang served as a visible symbol of the Horned God (which is especially fitting if one looks at the Devil as a corrupted version of earlier horned gods such as the Greek Pan). As someone who utilizes a stang on occasion during ritual, I can attest to the fact that it's a very powerful-looking ritual tool. I'm sure Cochrane saw it in a similar fashion since he often used his stang as a focal point during ritual. Many Witches who use the stang also decorate it to reflect the Wheel of the Year.

In addition to the stang, Cochrane used most of the "traditional" tools we associate with Witchcraft today, including the knife. Originally Cochrane referred to his blade as an athame,[20] like most Witches in the early 1960s. The word appears less frequently in his later writings, generally replaced by the more generic-sounding "knife." Most of those who follow the teachings of Cochrane today simply call their blades a "knife."

Cochrane used his knife in a way similar to that of the athame. It was used to enact the symbolic Great Rite and was said to represent masculine energy. It was also used to bless cakes and ale and to assist in the calling of the four elements. Cochrane-inspired covens (or *cuveens*) often share one "coven knife" during ritual. This is different from many Wiccan-style groups that encourage individual ownership of an athame. Indeed, I'm unaware of any Wiccan-style groups that share a coven athame like Cochrane's groups share the knife.

While there are many similarities between Cochrane's Traditional Witchcraft and modern Wicca, some of the ritual differences between the two are extremely interesting, and often involve the knife. As I wrote at the beginning of this chapter, there are many different types of Witchcraft labeled "traditional," but the strain I'm most familiar with is Cochrane's, so those are the rituals included in this book. All of the

---

20 John of Monmouth, with Gillian Spraggs and Shani Oates, *Genuine Witchcraft Is Explained: The Secret History of the Royal Windsor Coven and the Regency* (Somerset, UK: Capall Bann, 2012), p. 418.

. . .

The Knife in Traditional Witchcraft

rites included here were directly inspired by the writings of Cochrane himself and those who carry on his legacy.

Traditional Witchcraft Rituals with the Knife and the Sword

Traditional Witchcraft often operates with a different running order than other forms of Witchcraft. Instead of calling the quarters and casting the circle at the beginning of ritual, this happens toward the middle, after the Goddess and the God have been invoked. Most significantly, the knife is not used for casting the circle but is actively involved with the four quarters.

The knife is utilized in a more familiar way during the Great Rite and the blessing of the cakes and ale. Many of the "flourishes" in those rites are different from the ones previously shared in this book, but the ideas behind them are generally the same. All of the rituals outlined here can easily be adapted for use in more Wiccan-style rites.

Since this is not a book about Traditional Witchcraft, we will only be touching on rites that involve the knife or sword; but for those who want to dig a bit deeper, I feel as if I should offer an outline of Cochrane's rites. When Cochrane passed in 1966, he did so without leaving behind any detailed accounts of his working. As a result, those who practice his Craft rely on his letters and the works of those who performed ritual with him (Witches such as Evan John Jones and Doreen Valiente).

Using those sources, my Cochrane-inspired rites proceed in this order: fashioning the bridge, opening prayer, coven cleansing, blessing, placement of the stang and cauldron/call to the Goddess and the God, calling the quarters, casting the circle, working, cakes and ale, closing the circle, and finally, releasing the bridge. This is most certainly not how every Traditional Witch conducts their rituals, but it is my approximation after studying the letters of Cochrane. The bits in this book can be used to create a larger Traditional Witch ritual, or they can simply be inserted into more common forms of Craft. They are effective and offer an interesting change of pace for most Witches.

Instead of the terms *high priestess* and *high priest*, Cochrane used the terms *Maid* and *Magister*. Since those are what he used, it's what I'll be using here (even though my wife and high priestess does not like being referred to as a "Maid"—proceed with caution if you use that term). Many of the groups that emerged from the forge of Tubal Cain utilize other roles in their rituals, but for simplicity's sake I've kept everything between Maid and Magister. For those interested in Traditional Witchcraft, check out the bibliography and further reading list for more information.

Fashioning the Bridge

Cochrane's rituals were a journey into another realm, and he generally began his rituals by having the members of his coven walk over a symbolic bridge. His bridge was the pathway between the mundane world and the magical one, and signified entry into sacred space. That sacred space is sometimes referred to as the *Spiral Castle*, an idea taken from the book *The White Goddess* by the English poet Robert Graves (1895–1985).

Fashioning the bridge is a short rite, but an effective one, and generally gets the attention of everyone in the coven. Instead of beginning the ritual in a circle, the Magister and the Maid should stand at the threshold of the ritual space, with the coven outside that space looking in. When circumstances permit, the bridge should be located in the north, but that's not always possible. In my coven we create the bridge at our ritual room's entry point.[21]

The Magister should be carrying the coven sword and the Maid the broom. Maid and Magister should be focused on creating a pathway into magical space. When performing this rite, I try to imagine my sword glowing a little bit while

---

21 Evan John Jones and Doreen Valiente, *Witchcraft: A Tradition Renewed* (Custer, WA: Phoenix Publishing, 1990), p. 123. The ritual seen here is adapted from the work of Jones, along with some of Cochrane's letters as found in John of Monmouth's *Genuine Witchcraft Is Explained*.

charging it with magical energy. The Maid generally does the same.

Looking into the eyes of the coven, the Magister should dramatically hold up his sword and then set it down while saying:

> *I lay down this sword so that we*
> *might walk in other realms.*

The Maid holds her broom aloft and lays it over the sword, saying:

> *And I this broom. Conjoined and bound together,*
> *they represent the most ancient of magics.*

The Magister and Maid step back from the newly created bridge and bid the coven entrance into the rite. The Magister welcomes them in with the following words:

> *Step across this gate and come into the*
> *Otherworld, the Spiral Castle where all*
> *true Witches tread. So be it done!*

Once the bridge has been constructed, the ritual proceeds in whatever way the coven chooses. The Magister, Maid, and coven return to the bridge near the conclusion of the rite.

Once all the divine forces within the circle have been dismissed, the Magister and the Maid approach the bridge.

The Knife in Traditional Witchcraft

Slowly the Maid picks up the broom and holds it to her heart. The Magister then does the same with the sword. Looking into the eyes of the Maid, the Magister says:

That which was joined is now asunder.

The Maid replies:

The gate is now open. Let all who have journeyed into the mysteries be free to depart this place. So be it done!

The coven is now allowed to leave the ritual space and the rite is over.

Calling the Quarters

Invoking the four quarters in Cochrane's version of Traditional Witchcraft requires both a cauldron and an athame. Begin by filling the cauldron (if you don't have a copper or iron cauldron, a bowl also works) with fresh spring water from a pitcher or other large container. The Maid fills the cauldron while saying:

I fill this cauldron so we might glimpse the cauldron of Cerridwen that is the cup of life and immortality. Within her waters we begin our journey to the Otherworld, where true witchery dwells. We are the children of the Goddess and this cauldron is her symbol.

Instead of calling watchtowers or elemental energies, Cochrane called to four different gods at each of the cardinal points of the compass. He saw each of these gods as living in their own space (or castle). When invoked, they help Witches journey to the other side and walk between the worlds. In his cosmology, the elements of earth, air, and water are seen as feminine attributes; as a result, the Maid calls the gods there. The Magister calls to fire in the east.[22]

After each god is called, the Magister dips his knife into the cauldron and flips the water upon the blade toward each of the four quarters. I do this near the outside of the circle instead of in the middle by the altar. The "ritual walk" adds a bit of drama to the rite and ensures that the gods called to enter the circle in the proper space. Sharing the water from the Goddess cauldron at each of the four quarters symbolizes her power being necessary to move from one world to the next and adds some feminine energy to a rite focused mainly on four gods.

After the water is poured into the cauldron, the Magister and the Maid should stand in the center of the circle by the altar. The Magister begins the rite by saying:

22   Ann Finnin, *The Forge of Tubal Cain* (Sunland, CA: Pendraig Publishing, 2008), pp. 43–44. I'm indebted to Finnin's book for helping me find the gods behind the names. The ritual here is adapted from Finnin's book and Cochrane's letters.

The Knife in Traditional Witchcraft

We begin our journey at a castle in the east
surrounded by fire and ruled by Lacet.

The Magister then sticks his knife into the cauldron and walks to the east, flicking the water from the knife when he reaches the perimeter of the circle. This action is repeated at each of the cardinal points after the invocations to the gods are read.

Lacet is another name for *Lugh*, the shining one of Celtic myth. Here he is invoked as a god of the sun and of knowledge. Some writers have also linked him to Lucifer, a figure that often comes up in Traditional Witchcraft. This Lucifer is not the Christian Devil but another figure of wisdom.

The Magister now approaches the altar again. When he arrives, the Maid continues the rite by saying:

Our next journey is to a castle in the south
surrounded by forests of trees and ruled by Carenos.

Carenos here is a variant spelling of *Cernunnos*, the Gaulish-Celtic god of hunting and the natural world. Cernunnos is one of the most popular aspects of the Horned God.

The Maid and the Magister now turn to the west, where the god Nodens is invoked:

On to the west and a castle deep in
the ocean ruled by Nodens.

Nodens is a Celtic god native to the British Isles who is often associated with the sea and healing. Unlike the other gods who are a part of this rite, Nodens is not a variant spelling.

The final act of the rite is in the north, and again the Maid calls to the god being invoked:

> *And finally to the north and a castle built*
> *in the sky and ruled by Tettans.*

Tettans sounds very much like a group of fairies or people but is most likely an alternate spelling of *Toutais*, another Celtic deity (and one who has been known to show up in the French comic *Asterix*). He was generally seen as a god of protection and hunting and was often seen as similar to the Greek god Hermes. That's possibly why he shows up here associated with the element of air.

I've found no "quarter dismissal" in the works of Cochrane equal to the calls shared here. If you want to dismiss the energies called here in a symbolic way, I suggest starting in the north. Have the Magister walk to the cardinal point and then hold aloft his knife while the Maid says:

> *We now leave behind the castle in*
> *the sky and its ruler, Tettans.*

The Magister then walks back to the cauldron and ceremonially shakes the water collected there back into the cauldron.

This process is then repeated at the rest of the quarters, with the Maid offering the appropriate dismissals: *We now leave behind the castle in the ocean and its ruler, Nodens. We now leave behind the castle surrounded by forests ruled by Carenos.* The Magister "collects" the water he shared at each of the cardinal points and then "returns" it to the cauldron. Finally the Magister says:

> *We now leave behind the castle of*
> *fire and its ruler, Lacet.*

He then approaches the east and walks back to the cauldron.

After the rulers of the castles have been dismissed, the water in the cauldron is then either spilled upon the ground or returned to the pitcher it came from. Then pitcher is taken outside and the water shared with the earth at the ritual's conclusion. The Maid then says:

> *From the earth it came and from the earth*
> *it will return when we depart this place. In*
> *the name of the Goddess, so be it done!*

The Great Rite/Cakes and Ale

Symbolically there's no difference between the Great Rite as practiced in Cochrane's Craft and the one practiced in Wicca. There are some slight changes in the ritual, and many of those changes involve how the athame as used. For this rite you will need a knife, cup, sharpening stone, and mirror. If the ritual is inside, you'll also need a lantern or candle. The cup should contain whatever beverage you are using for cakes and ale. Since Cochrane used the cup's content to symbolize blood and sacrifice, the drink should be red, preferably red wine or cranberry juice.

The rite starts with the Maid picking up the cup and, if indoors, the mirror. The Magister stands beside her with his knife and the candle (or lantern). The Maid then holds the mirror near the cup's rim, angled to reflect the light of the candle into the cup. The Magister holds the candle up near the mirror and says to the Maid:

> *I bring you the light of the moon.*

The Maid replies:

> *For it brings us the light of the Lady.*

(If the ritual is outdoors, the Magister picks up the mirror and uses it to reflect the moon's light into the cup.)

As the light reflects into the cup, the Maid calls to the Goddess and reflects on the Great Rite:

> *Great Goddess, I call to you now in our ritual to*
> *tear apart the veil that separates us. The knife*
> *is to the male; the cup is to the female. Joined*
> *together, they symbolize new possibilities and the*

continuation of all life. This cup is a symbol of
your abundance; the knife symbolizes the phallic
power of the Horned One, your lover and loved.

The Magister then sets down the candle (or mirror, if outdoors) and picks up a sharpening stone while saying:

Horned One, join us in the charging of this
drink. In your union with the Great Goddess,
the two of you become one and reveal to us life's
mysteries. By drinking from this cup may we
experience the grace and mysteries of the gods.

The Magister then sharpens his knife three times upon the sharpening stone before plunging it into the cup. The knife is then used to stir the contents of the cup three times. When this is complete, he splashes a bit of the wine at each of the four cardinal points, beginning in the east and proceeding clockwise (south, west, and finally north).

When the Magister returns to the center altar, he and the Maid kiss and then say in unison, *So be it done.* Then they both drink from the cup. The Maid then sets down the cup and picks up the plate of cakes (or bread, or whatever you choose to eat during ritual). The Maid stands in front of the Magister in a pose suggesting that she is offering the cakes to him and says:

Maid holding the cup while the
Magister sharpens his blade nearby

239

> *I call to the Old Gods that they might look upon this*
> *bread and witness our sacrifice unto them. This gift is*
> *given to the gods and to those of this coven so that we*
> *might better understand the mysteries. As Witches,*
> *this is our right and privilege. By the call of blood to*
> *blood, we eat and share this bread. So be it done!*

The Magister then takes his knife and touches each cake with the point while saying:

> *Through the power of this knife*
> *We are led to knowledge and life.*
> *The Lady shares with us the grain*
> *Reaped from the earth with joy and pain.*
> *From the ground and dust this bread came*
> *And to that ground will be for us the same.*
> *But from death also comes rebirth,*
> *As it ever is upon the earth!*
> *In the names of they who are one,*
> *We Witches all say, be it done!*

Then the Maid and the Magister each take a piece of bread from the plate and eat it. The plate is then handed back to the Magister while the Maid takes the cup. Before leaving to distribute the wine and bread to the rest of the coven, they stare into each other's eyes and say:

In the Old One's name we eat this bread
With great terror and fearful dread.
We drink this in our Lady's name,
And she'll gather us home again. [23]

After all have drank from the cup and eaten the bread, the ritual proceeds. Be sure to save some bread and wine to offer the gods when your ritual is over. If the rite is outdoors, this can be left on the ground during the ceremony. If the ritual is indoors, it should be done once the rite has ended.

GETTING TO THE POINT
Jenya T. Beachy

THERE IS A line of Witchcraft born on the West Coast of the United States only nominally influenced by the goings-on in Europe. That tradition is known as the Feri Tradition and was

---

23 According to Michael Howard that bit of rhyme is from an old "Scottish Craft Source." Michael Howard, *Robert Cochrane The Magister of the Clan*, from "Pagan Dawn" magazine, Lammas 2007. It appears in Doreen Valiente's *The Rebirth of Witchcraft*, Phoenix Publishing, 1989, pg. 123.

The Knife in Traditional Witchcraft

begun by Victor and Cora Anderson. Today there are many different traditions in the Feri family tree.

In the Shapeshifter line of Feri Tradition, there is a focus on relationships and perspective; we understand that all things have their corollary within us. Our skin is a point of reference from which the universe expands and contracts, from the infinitesimally small to the immeasurably big. The edge of us separates the interior world from the exterior world and is the blade of our individuality, shaping our lives as we go.

The Witch's knife is a tool of power. To wield it safely, we must become adept at managing our own power. We take responsibility for our part in the circumstances of our lives. We sort what is within us from what is outside of us. We attend to our complexes, and the blade assists us in that work.

Our knife is a real device of cutting, of separating this thing from that, and it is dangerous. You might cut away something you did not intend to part from. You might hurt someone.

There is nothing inherently wrong with this.

Sometimes we must be rebroken so that we can heal up right this time. Sometimes we must open a wound to let the infection drain. We need sunlight and air on our hurts to help them heal. The knife can open a path for that light to travel. The knife can be the path, reflective and clean.

We understand the value of being sharp and flexible so we can point and thrust with confidence. To have this confidence, we learn to know ourselves. The cultivation of our will allows us to stand in the fires of our complexes, trusting that we will survive.

The knife is the tool of will.

Meditating on the events in our lives that have burned us, pounded us, folded us, reminds us that adversity shapes us. Recalling the cool relief of the gods' sweet waters reminds us that both ease and challenge are gifts they give their children.

The knife can support, keeping the back straight and shoulders square. It aligns itself to the body and we may walk with the blade against our backbone, providing us with a framework.

The knife can defend. Laid across the threshold, it keeps intruders away. Worn on the belt, it reminds us that we are capable of doing what is needed.

When walking into the circle, carry the Witch's blade, and leave the shield at the door. Enter sacred space unencumbered by defensiveness. But always come with power. And recognize the power of brothers and sisters of the Craft.

Blessed be your strength.

Jenya T. Beachy
www.jenyatbeachy.com

The Knife in Traditional Witchcraft

Epilogue

The Circle Is Open,
The Book Is Over

Every time I pick up my athame, I like to stop and think about the millions of people over the centuries who have wielded their blades as magical instruments. In those moments I'm linked to prehistoric humankind, the great pagan religions of ancient Europe, and medieval conjurers. The athame is more than just a link to the past; it's a vital and very much a living part of Witchcraft today.

When I gather with other Witches at festivals, talk often turns to our athames. Sometimes we sound like proud parents discussing our children during such moments. "My athame was made by so and so," someone might chime in. Another person will tell of how they just knew their athame was perfect the first time they picked it up. Witches take pride in many things, but the athame always seems to be their most prized magical possession.

I love my chalices, deity statues, and even my broom, but I've never wanted to sleep next to those things. I've wanted to take my athame with me everywhere, and only the good sense of my wife has stopped that from happening over the years. Our blades often reflect aspects of our personalities too. Some of the most powerful Witches I know use very basic athames, but that always seems to reflect who they are. A truly powerful Witch needs no extra adornment.

If there's one thing you take from this book, I hope it's the knowledge that your athame, and your use of it, really comes down to you. There are traditions, history, and lore about knives and athames, but what truly makes a tool is how we use it individually as Witches. In the long-term scheme of things, there is no absolute right or wrong when it comes to the athame, but only what's right for you, the individual Witch.

In my twenty years of Witchcraft, I've gone from being wary of the athame to falling in love with it. My athames are now among my most prized possessions, and when I pass from this earth I hope that another Witch will pick them up so that a little bit of my energy might remain in the magick circle. Happy conjuring!

Appendix
One

Theban Script

A	B	C	D	E	F	G
A	B	C	D	E	F	G
H	I	J	K	L	M	N
O	P	Q	R	S	T	U
V	W	X	Y	Z	END	

Appendix Two

Elder Futhark Runes

ᚢ URUZ: strength, healing, will

ᛟ OTHEL: inheritance, possessions, help

ᚨ ANSUZ: advice, speech, wisdom

ᚷ GIFU: partnership, love, gifts

ᛗ MANNAZ: cooperation, humankind, seek advice

ᛉ EOLH: protection, friendship, premonition

ᛇ EIHWAZ: defense, delay, obstacle

ᛝ ING: success, relief, milestones

ᚾ NIED: patience, delay, learning

ᚲ PERDRO: secrets, surprises, mysteries

ᛏ TIR: male, strength, motivation

ᚲ KENAZ: hearth, power, opening up

ᛇ JERA: rewards, karma, legalities

ᚹ WUNJO: well-being, happiness, joy

ᚠ FEHU: fulfillment, material gain, money

ᚱ RAIDHO: journey, strategy, movement

ᚺ HAGALL: limitation, delays, disruption

ᛚ LAGAZ: female, intuition, imagination

ᛗ EHWAZ: physical movement, travel

ᛒ BEORC: family, birth, new love

ᛋ SIGEL: victory, power, success

ᛁ ISA: cessation, standstill, perfidy, freeze

ᛗ DAEG: breakthrough, growth, radical change

ᚦ THURISAZ: luck, awakening, thorn

(BLANK) WYRD: fate, trust, unknowable

Bibliography and Further Reading

I've been reading Pagan books for as long as I've been a Pagan. Most of them say very little about athames, but I found the following books useful during the writing of this book. They are listed in alphabetical order according to author.

Buckland's Complete Book of Witchcraft by Raymond Buckland. St. Paul, MN: Llewellyn Publications, 1994. Updated and expanded in 2002.

I don't agree with everything Buckland writes, but this book had a huge impact on me as a young Witch. As a training tool, there are few better books.

The Robert Cochrane Letters by Robert Cochrane and Evan John Jones, with Michael Howard (editor). Somerset, UK: Capall Bann, 2002.

Nearly all of Cochrane's letters are now available for free online, but this edition contains some nifty notes by Howard that further illuminate them. Cochrane wrote to confuse, so take his letters with a large pentacle of salt.

Grimoires: A History of Magic Books by Owen Davies. New York: Oxford University Press, 2009.

The grimoire tradition and ceremonial magic had a huge impact on modern Witchcraft. Davies's book doesn't explicitly trace that history, but it's easy to spot if one knows what one is looking for.

Wicca: Magickal Beginnings: A Study of the Possible Origins of the Rituals and Practices Found in This Modern Tradition of Pagan Witchcraft and Magick by Sorita d'Este and David Rankine. London: Avalonia, 2008.

Wicca contains the most comprehensive breakdown of Wiccan tools and ritual I've ever encountered on the printed page. This is a hidden gem of a book that should be on every Witch's bookshelf.

A Witches' Bible: The Complete Witches' Handbook by Janet and Stewart Farrar. Custer, WA: Phoenix Publishing, 1996. Originally published in two separate volumes as *The Witches' Way* (1984) and *Eight Sabbats For Witches* (1988).

The best and most complete introduction to British Traditional–style Witchcraft on the market. Some of the material they include lacks context, but overall this is a superb book.

The Forge of Tubal Cain by Ann Finnin. Sunland, CA: Pendraig Publishing, 2008.

Finnin takes Robert Cochrane's material and adds her own spin to it, and she does a great job of breaking down his ritual and making it a little easier to digest.

High Magic's Aid by Gerald Gardner. Originally published in 1949. Available today from a variety of publishers.

This book is significant for a number of reasons. The word *athame* first appears in its pages, but perhaps more importantly, Gardner spends more time writing about the athame in *High Magic's Aid* than in his two nonfiction books about Witchcraft.

Witchcraft Today and *The Meaning of Witchcraft* by Gerald Gardner. Originally published in 1954 and 1959, respectively. Available today from various publishers.

Gardner's two nonfiction books about Witchcraft are not all that readable today but are still noteworthy because of their historical significance.

Witchcraft: A Tradition Renewed by Evan John Jones and Doreen Valiente. Custer, WA: Phoenix Publishing, 1990.

This is the best primer on Cochrane-style Craft ever written. Jones was a member of the original clan and, in many ways, Cochrane's successor.

The Roebuck in the Thicket: An Anthology of the Robert Cochrane Witchcraft Tradition by Evan John Jones and Robert Cochrane, with Michael Howard (editor). Somerset, UK: Capall Bann, 2001.

Most of this is by Jones, and in it he breaks down Cochrane's system piece by piece.

Magical Religion and Modern Witchcraft edited by James R. Lewis. Albany, NY: State University of New York Press, 1996. Most notably the article "White Witches: Historic Fact and Romantic Fantasy" by James W. Baker.

Baker's article touches on a number of fascinating things and might be the best part of *Magical Religion*. The entire volume is notable for being one of the first academic books almost completely about modern Paganism.

Early Mormonism and the Magic World View by D. Michael
Quinn. Salt Lake City, UT: Signature Books, 1998.

Much of this book is of little interest to most Pagans, but Quinn's history of magick and the occult in early America is unsurpassed.

The Mysteries and Secrets of Magic by C. J. S. Thompson.
New York: Causeway Books, 1973. Originally published in 1927 and subsequently in many various editions.

Thompson's book is mostly a how-to volume on ceremonial magic. It is noteworthy because of its use of the words *arthany* and *arthana*.

The Rebirth of Witchcraft by Doreen Valiente. Custer, WA:
Phoenix Publishing, 1989.

Valiente's book is one of the most important ever written on the history of the Craft, and the best chapter in it is on Robert Cochrane.

GET MORE AT LLEWELLYN.COM

Visit us online to browse hundreds of our books and decks, plus sign up to receive our e-newsletters and exclusive online offers.

- • Free tarot readings • Spell-A-Day • Moon phases
- • Recipes, spells, and tips • Blogs • Encyclopedia
- • Author interviews, articles, and upcoming events

GET SOCIAL WITH LLEWELLYN

Find us on
Facebook
www.Facebook.com/LlewellynBooks

Follow us on

www.Twitter.com/Llewellynbooks

GET BOOKS AT LLEWELLYN

LLEWELLYN ORDERING INFORMATION

 Order online: Visit our website at www.llewellyn.com to select your books and place an order on our secure server.

 Order by phone:
- • Call toll free within the U.S. at 1-877-NEW-WRLD (1-877-639-9753)
- • Call toll free within Canada at 1-866-NEW-WRLD (1-866-639-9753)
- • We accept VISA, MasterCard, and American Express

Order by mail:
Send the full price of your order (MN residents add 6.875% sales tax) in U.S. funds, plus postage and handling to: Llewellyn Worldwide, 2143 Wooddale Drive, Woodbury, MN 55125-2989

POSTAGE AND HANDLING:
STANDARD: (U.S. & Canada)
(Please allow 12 business days)
$25.00 and under, add $4.00.
$25.01 and over, FREE SHIPPING.

INTERNATIONAL ORDERS (airmail only):
$16.00 for one book, plus $3.00 for each additional book.

Visit us online for more shipping options.
Prices subject to change.

FREE CATALOG!

To order, call
1-877-
NEW-WRLD
ext. 8236
or visit our
website

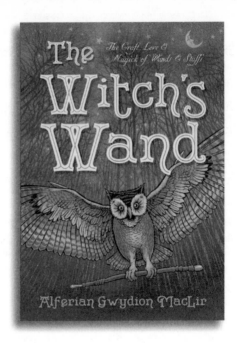

The Witch's Wand
The Craft, Lore, and Magick of Wands & Staffs
Alferian Gwydion MacLir

Discover the fascinating history, symbolism, and modern use of the wand with this comprehensive guide by professional wand-maker Alferian Gwydion MacLir. From a variety of spells and rituals to methods for making your own wand, *The Witch's Wand* presents a wealth of knowledge that every age and every kind of witch can use.

978-0-7387-4195-6, 264 pp., 5 x 7   **$15.99**

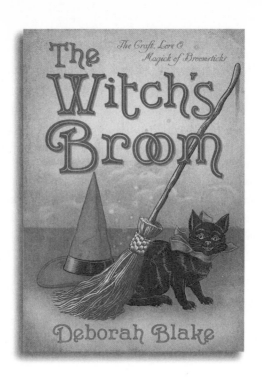

The Craft, Lore &
Magick of Broomsticks

The Witch's Broom

Deborah Blake

The Witch's Broom
The Craft, Lore & Magick of Broomsticks
DEBORAH BLAKE

From besoms to broomcorn, Deborah Blake takes you on a magickal flight into the history and lore of broomsticks and the witches who use them.

Throughout the ages, brooms and witches have always been thought of as a united, inseparable pair. Whether being used to sweep your home or help with your magickal endeavors, the broom is a more versatile and useful tool than you've ever imagined. You'll enjoy special segments entitled "Real Witches, Real Brooms" that feature well-known witchy authors sharing their personal uses of broomsticks. Whether you want to add a new facet to your magick practice, make a unique gift for someone special, or explore the role of brooms in Witchcraft's past and present, *The Witch's Broom* is your perfect guide.

978-0-7387-3802-4, 304 pp., 5 x 7   **$15.99**

TIMOTHY RODERICK

WICCA

ANOTHER YEAR AND A DAY

366 DAYS OF MAGICAL PRACTICE
IN THE CRAFT OF THE WISE

Wicca: Another Year and a Day
366 Days of Magical Practice in the Craft of the Wise
TIMOTHY RODERICK

Expand your understanding of Wicca and Witchcraft, gain greater spiritual insight, and learn ways to boost your magical potential with this step-by-step guide. In his follow-up to *Wicca: A Year and A Day,* author Timothy Roderick presents various ways to cultivate your spirituality and become an adept in the Old Ways.

978-0-7387-4550-3, 360 pp., 8 x 10   **$29.99**

To order, call 1-877-NEW-WRLD
Prices subject to change without notice
Order at Llewellyn.com 24 hours a day, 7 days a week!

"I love Jane Meredith's focus on local magic . . . [She's] a true originator of
approaches to magic and spirit that can inspire us in these times."—STARHAWK

CIRCLE
of EIGHT

Creating Magic for Your Place on Earth

Jane Meredith

Circle of Eight
Creating Magic for Your Place on Earth
JANE MEREDITH

Circle of Eight is an exciting new approach to magic that is based on your geography, your climate, and your experiences. *Circle of Eight* can be used to celebrate the Festivals of the Wheel of the Year; to create an on-going ritual group; and to explore and develop magical relationship with the land around you. Providing instructions on how to set up your own Circle of Eight and stories illustrating important magical principles, the *Circle of Eight* radically re-invents our relationship to traditional circle magic. Suitable for beginners seeking ritual and magic that are relevant to them as well as advanced practitioners, this book helps you step deeply into the powerful magic of the directions and the great Wheel of the Year.

978-0-7387-4215-1, 312 pp., 6 x 9   **$17.99**

Llewellyn's Sabbat Essentials

OSTARA

Rituals, Recipes & Lore for the Spring Equinox

Ostara

Rituals, Recipes & Lore for the Spring Equinox
Llewellyn and Kerri Connor

Llewellyn's Sabbat Essentials series explores the old and new ways of celebrating the seasonal rites that are the cornerstones in the witch's year.

A well-rounded introduction to Ostara, this attractive book features rituals, recipes, lore, and correspondences. It includes hands-on information for modern celebrations, spells and divination, recipes and crafts, invocations and prayers, and more!

Ostara—also known as the Spring Equinox—is a time of renewal, a time to plant seeds as the earth once again comes to life. This guide to the history and modern celebration of Ostara shows you how to perform rituals and work magic to energize yourself and renew the power and passion to live and grow.

978-0-7387-4181-9, 240 pp., 5 x 7   **$11.99**

To Write to the Author

If you wish to contact the author or would like more information about this book, please write to the author in care of Llewellyn Worldwide and we will forward your request. Both the author and the publisher appreciate hearing from you and learning of your enjoyment of this book and how it has helped you. Llewellyn Worldwide cannot guarantee that every letter written to the author can be answered, but all will be forwarded. Please write to:

Jason Mankey

Llewellyn Worldwide

2143 Wooddale Drive

Woodbury, MN 55125-2989

Please enclose a self-addressed stamped envelope for reply
or $1.00 to cover costs. If outside the USA, enclose
an international postal reply coupon.

Many of Llewellyn's authors have websites with additional information and resources. For more information, please visit our website:

WWW.LLEWELLYN.COM